Praise for Patrick Henry Hansen's

From Great Moments in History™ Series

"Patrick's link between history and sales is very entertaining, but more importantly, very relevant to modern sales and marketing professionals. If you are interested in dramatically improving sales results, read these books."

—Dr. Stephen R. Covey, author of,
The 7 Habits of Highly Effective People

"These exciting books of superb selling methods and techniques, told against a vast panorama of historical events, are not only entertaining, they also show sales people specific ways to double their sales and double their income."

—Brian Tracy, author of, *The Psychology of Selling*

"Patrick's use of history to teach modern methods of sales and marketing is remarkable—an inspiring, captivating read."

—Larry King, host, CNN's *The Larry King Show*

"Patrick's understanding of sales, together with his wit, makes his book series extremely enjoyable and informative. I've been lucky enough to see some of his ideas applied to a sales organization. As a result, pipelines grew, morale improved and our sales team performed better than ever. I strongly recommend his books and training programs."

—Kyle Powell, Co-founder, Novell

"Bravo... a maverick approach to sales and marketing. Patrick's use of history is engaging, interesting, and informative—a blueprint for sales and marketing success."

—Gerhard Gschwandtner, founder of *Selling Power Magazine*

"Patrick reminds us that those who ignore history are condemned to repeat it. His use of classic scenarios informs present day practitioners. He communicates solid marketing principles, helping readers understand the past in an unforgettable manner."

—Dr. William D. Danko, co-author of the best-selling, *The Millionaire Next Door,* & Chair of the Marketing Department at the State University of New York

"These are fantastic books. Not only are the sales concepts and marketing principles profound, but the manner in which they are communicated is totally unique. I strongly recommend these books."

—Hyrum W. Smith, Vice Chairman of the Board, FranklinCovey Co. and author of *The 10 Natural Laws of Successful Time and Life Management*

"Fantastic! If you're interested in dramatically improving communication skills and sales results, learn from the masters of the past by reading these books."

—Ron McMillan, Coauthor of the New York Times Bestsellers *Crucial Conversations* and *Crucial Confrontations.*

"In a word... WOW! An irreplaceable tool in the sales process, these books will make you a more impactful, learned, and skilled professional. As someone who facilitates management and leadership development, I found that the examples in this book even apply beyond the sales process. They are lessons for life. If only we all had the oratory skills of Winston Churchill, Mark Twain, or Thomas Jefferson. This book is a huge step in that direction!"

—Clark Jones, Corporate Trainer, Sinclair Oil Corporation

"Every day I have to sell my political opinions in the arena of ideas. Rarely does someone capture so many priceless truths of communication in such an interesting way. Patrick's use of history as a teaching tool is fabulous."

—Rob Bishop, United States Congressman

"Finally someone has organized and conceptualized the selling process. Loaded with historical facts, how to examples and practical strategies, this book is a step-by-step guide for dramatically increasing sales."

—Kurt Mortensen, Author of *Maximum Influence*

"Simply the most unique books I've read on sales and marketing. Patrick's use of history to teach modern methods of sales and marketing is informative and inspiring."

—Robert Dilenschneider, Author of *Moses: CEO*

Also by Patrick Henry Hansen

From Great Moments in History™ Series:

Power Prospecting: Cold Calling Strategies for Modern-day Sales People

The DNASelling Method: Selling Strategies for Modern-day Sales People

Sales-Side Negotiation: Negotiation Strategies for Modern-day Sales People

Winning Sales Presentations

From Great Moments in History

Winning Sales Presentations

PRESENTATION STRATEGIES FOR MODERN-DAY SALES PEOPLE

Patrick Henry Hansen

BRAVE PUBLISHING, INC.

Second Edition

Brave Publishing, Inc. Alpine, Utah.

ISBN 1-932908-11-0

The *From Great Moments in History* series is available at quantity discounts. For more information, please contact Patrick Henry & Associates:

Toll-Free (877) 204-4341
Fax (877) 204-4341
www.PatrickHenryInc.com

Author Patrick Henry Hansen may be contacted as follows:
Email: patrick@PatrickHenryInc.com

Dedicated To

❧ My son, Adam—future presenter extraordinaire. And to my four daughters: Alexis, Savannah, Bronwyn and Aryanna—for inspiring me to focus on what really matters in life. ❧

Acknowledgements

Special thanks to Matthew and Heather Moore for their meticulous editing skills, principle development, and insightful content review, and to my colleagues, Brian Tracy and Dr. William Danko, for their professional critique and personal support. Thanks to Larry Brooks, Darren Dibb, Kevin Dibb, Zac Fenton, Parker Garlitz, Leland McCay, Clint Sanderson, and David Stephens—some of the most gifted presentation professionals I know, for their insight and "in the trenches" feedback.

Contents

Figures

Historical References

- Sir Winston Churchill inspires the British Empire to fight against The Third Reich. (v)
- Southern general George Pickett opines about the Confederacy's defeat at Gettysburg. (1)
- President Kennedy delivers one of the most memorable inaugural addresses in U.S. history. (7)
- British officers concoct a scheme of deception to dupe the Germans into fortifying Greece instead of Sicily during the Allied invasion of Europe during WWII. (10)
- Joan of Arc gains the support of King Charles. (20)
- Francis Crick and James Watson make the most profound scientific discovery of the twentieth century—the structure of DNA. (23)
- Queen Elizabeth issues a political treatise providing rationale for intervening on behalf of Dutch Protestants in their war against Spain. (27)
- Julius Caesar battles German chieftain Ariovistus. (40)
- British mathematicians and chess players decipher *Enigma*, a machine to decipher German communication codes. (43)
- Meriwether Lewis and William Clark use a pre-expedition questionnaire to acquire information about the native cultures and geography of their Northwest journey. (55)
- Roman priest Augustine converts King Ethelbert and the Anglo Saxons of England to Christianity. (58)
- Pericles persuades Athenian warriors to battle the Spartans. (75)
- Johann Sebastian Bach, Wolfgang Amadeus Mozart, and Ludwig van Beethoven create the most famous music in history. (86)
- French baron Pierre de Coubertin reinstates the Olympic Games as a means of preparing his countrymen for war with Germany. (96)
- Margaret Thatcher delivers a thunderous speech to the House of Commons concerning the Argentine invasion of the Falkland Islands. (103)
- Meriwether Lewis and William Clark use dress and appearance to impress and intimidate native tribes. (105)
- President William Henry Harrison presents the longest inaugural address in U.S. history. (113)

- President Abraham Lincoln delivers the most famous speech in U.S. history—the Gettysburg address. (123)
- Sergeant York single-handedly captures 132 Germans in WWI. (129)
- The Lewis and Clark expedition uses a bow swivel gun to demonstrate the fire power and advanced weaponry of the United States. (132)
- Queen Elizabeth I inspires her troops to defeat the Spanish Armada. (140)
- The Soviet Union stuns America by launching the first space traveler: a dog named Laika who died in orbit. (142)
- Queen Elizabeth I reprimands a long-winded preacher. (143)
- Patrick Henry ignites the American Revolution against Great Britain with his "Liberty or Death" speech. (155)
- Mark Twain recounts his travels to the Sandwich Islands. (160)
- Bill Gates convinces IBM to use Microsoft's operating system. (162)
- Queen Elizabeth I masters the art of communication. (169)
- The Japanese News Agency mistranslates Premier Suzuki's statement concerning the surrender of Japanese troops leading to President Truman's decision to use atomic bombs. (171)
- Christopher Columbus gains the support of King Ferdinand and Queen Isabella. (175)
- Roman consul Marcus Cicero prevents the violent overthrow of the Roman Senate. (187)
- The Clinton Administration invents a political tactic called "Triangulation." (193)
- The Confederate Torpedo Bureau develops a disguised boiler room bomb. (195)
- Ethiopian leader Haile Selassie's dignified address overcomes Italian opposition at the League of Nations. (197)
- Benjamin Disraeli, Winston Churchill, and Alexander Hamilton Stephens use intelligent retorts to silence their critics. (206)
- Sojouner Truth questions Frederick Douglas at an abolitionist meeting. (209)
- George Washington's character prevents a military coup d'état of

the American government. (211)
- Nathan Rothschild uses Napoleon's defeat at the battle of Waterloo to enrich his family dynasty. (223)
- Moses receives The Ten Commandments from Jehovah. (231)
- Demosthenes delivers an oratorical masterpiece entitled *On the Crown* and becomes the greatest orator of Classical Greece. (232)
- Celtic Warriors battle Roman infantry using charioteer methods of warfare. (240)
- Robert Bruce defeats King Edward II at the battle of Bannockburn. (243)
- Benjamin Franklin develops a self-improvement system. (246)
- Abraham Lincoln experiences nine political defeats before being elected President of The United States. (250)

For more information regarding historic references, see the Selected Bibliography.

Introduction

In the opening year of World War II, Hitler traversed Europe like a giant colossus. His blitzkrieg tactics defeated Norway, smashed Holland and Belgium, and shattered the defense lines of France. After crushing the French, Hitler entered Paris as a military conqueror.

Not all was well, though, for the Nazi Fuehrer. As in the Napoleonic era, the shadow of Britain stood in the way of final victory. Hitler knew his conquests would be short lived without neutralizing Britain. The battle for France was over, but the battle for Britain had yet to be won. Hitler sent Britain an ultimatum for peace in an attempt to win, through negotiation, what he feared he would not be able to achieve without a costly war. "I am not the vanquished seeking favors, but the victor speaking in the name of reason." He called for "common-sense peace through negotiations." Hitler wanted recognition of his conquests, the return of Germany's colonies, and acceptance of his role as the arbiter of European affairs. Above all, he demanded the ousting of his verbal nemesis, Winston Churchill.

Considering the superiority of the German war machine, perhaps it would have been wise for the British to accept Hitler's offer. British allies had fallen victim one by one to the Nazi ruler. British forces had been routed in Norway, and British troops in France had been forced into the sea at Dunkirk. Britain's military was unprepared, and the will of the British people to carry out a continental war was in question. Britain was in a precarious position.

To the demanding Fuehrer, the British government responded with contemptuous silence.

At this moment of crisis, the lonely voice of leadership fell on one man—Winston Churchill. Winston Churchill had been a watchful student of the rise of Adolf Hitler and the Third Reich. He had continually warned British Prime Minister Neville Chamberlain and other British officials of the emptiness of Hitler's treaties. He was the most outspoken critic of Hitler throughout the

Fuehrer's rise to power. He alone was tasked with convincing the British people to resist, at all costs, the imposing threats of the Third Reich. An entire nation needed to be mobilized and convinced of a military call to action.

At the pinnacle of this crisis, Winston Churchill stepped up.

> I expect that the battle of Britain is about to begin. Upon this battle depends the survival of Christian civilization. Upon it depends our British way of life, and the long continuity of our institutions and our Empire. The whole fury and might of the enemy must very soon be turned on us. Hitler knows that he will have to break us in this island or lose the war. If we can stand up to him, all Europe may be free and the life of the world may move forward into broad, sunlit uplands. But if we fail, then the whole world, including the United States, including all that we have known and cared for, will sink into the abyss of a new Dark Age...
>
> Let us brace ourselves to our duties and so bear ourselves that, if the British Empire and its Commonwealth last for a thousand years, men will still say, "This was their finest hour."

Winston Churchill's defiant speech rallied the British will to fight. His presentation to the House of Commons was broadcast to millions of people and inspired British resolve to stand alone, if they must, and battle the Nazis. His oratory, language, and eloquence changed the course of world history forever. In one of history's most pivotal moments, Winston Churchill delivered one of the most celebrated presentations of all time.

Historic Presentations with Modern Application

Too many countries, too many businesses have been destroyed by not studying history.

—Donald Trump

Winston Churchill's 1940 speech to the House of Commons contains elements of both ancient and modern presentations. All of the contemporary elements of a successful presentation are present in his brief but historic speech—a strong introduction, powerful message, and clear call to action.

All great moments in history involve great speeches. All major historic events involve key figures involved in epic presentations, from the ancient oratory of Pericles, to the parliamentary rhetoric of Oliver Cromwell. The speeches of Cicero and Socrates are studied in universities even today. Modern history is dominated by presentations aimed at mass persuasion. Following the terrorist attacks of September 11th, 2001, President George W. Bush delivered an address to Congress that convinced even his most ardent Democratic opponents to politically rally behind his anti-terrorist agenda.

George Santayana said, "Those who cannot remember the past are condemned to repeat it." Sir Francis Bacon remarked, "Histories make men wise; poets witty; the mathematics subtle; natural philosophy deep." Cicero observed, "To be ignorant of what happened before you were born is to remain forever a child." Most of us have heard these quotes, but how many of us can actually recall specific lessons of the past and apply them to our personal and business lives? What can we take from the "there and then" and use in the "here and now?" We may know of the decadence of Rome, the arrogance of the French aristocracy, and the brutality of Stalin's regime, but what can we learn from this knowledge that can help us in business?

Actually, a great deal. Behind these events are great lessons of history. Whether they are small or epic, history's stories provide instruction of immense importance. Embodied in historic presentations, for example, are components of both structure and delivery. The great speeches of the past are textbooks for students of modern presentations. If you want to deliver a successful presentation, learn from the masters of the past.

Because history is such an excellent teacher, I reference numerous historical events throughout this book. Every chapter in each of the *From Great Moments in History* series begins with an historic speech or event that illustrates a particular point or principle. These historical events and experiences demonstrate presentation styles, techniques, and ideas that modern-day presenters can learn from.

"Their Finest Hour"

Presentations, as the apex of the sales process, determine who wins and who loses. Poor presentations rarely lead to won sales. Excellent presentations rarely lead to lost sales. The presentation is the "put-up-or-shut-up" section of the sale. More than at any other time of the sale, sellers demonstrate their ability to perform during the presentation.

Presentation and communication skills are the currency of successful selling. Studies show that sellers can be average in every other part of the sales process and still be very successful if they make powerful presentations. Whether dealing with an individual or a committee, a seller's ability to transmit ideas in a coherent and compelling fashion is one of the most important sales skills he or she must develop. It's a basic survival skill in the sales arena. The presentation is, and must be, a salesperson's "finest hour."

The Purpose of This Book

The purpose of this book is to instruct sellers in the science of delivering exceptional presentations. Although its principles are applicable for all types of presentations, it is specifically written for sales professionals. Its contents provide sellers with a structured process and clear methodology for delivering successful presentations and avoiding unnecessary pitfalls. By utilizing the concepts outlined in *Winning Sales Presentations*, sellers develop the confidence and expertise to successfully implement intelligent presentation strategies, deliver high impact presentations, and win more sales.

Presentation Types

Although it would be impossible to categorize every presentation type, most presentations can be categorized under the following classifications:

1. Podium Presentations
2. Platform Presentations
3. Business-To-Business Presentations
4. Business-To-Consumer Presentations

Podium presentations are typically formal presentations given from a stationary podium. The presenter is usually "glued" to the podium with little or no room to physically move around a room. Although podium presentations are popular (and in most cases effective) for formal business settings, religious meetings, political speeches, graduations, shareholder meetings, and educational addresses, they are the least effective format for making sales because they limit a speaker's ability to physically interact with an audience. Podium presentations are also not designed to address small numbers of people, which is a common sales situation.

Platform presentations differ from podium presentations because they are less physically restrictive. These presentations are typically semi-formal and provide presenters with a broad space or platform on which to physically maneuver. The platform presentation is often referred to as a "seminar" presentation. Most seminar companies use a banquet room or stage to address large audiences because it provides presenters with mobility. This encourages crowd interaction and enhances the visual aspects of a presentation. Platform presentations are popular formats for group presentations, trainings, and motivational speeches. Motivational speaker Tony Robbins is an example of a person who conducts platform presentations.

Business-to-business presentations are normally delivered on site at a prospect's location in offices, boardrooms, and conference rooms—anywhere that is feasible to demonstrate and discuss the product or service being offered. These presentations are typically delivered to committees consisting of two to ten people. Committee-based presentations are far more complex than individual based presentations because the needs of the committee are diverse and differ from one member to the next. For instance, if a committee consists of a CEO, CFO, and vice president of marketing, each member will have different needs and objectives and will evaluate the good or service from differing perspectives. The CEO will, more than likely, focus on return on investment. The CFO will be interested in the actual cost of the product. On the other hand, the vice president of marketing will want to know whether or not the product or service will help increase sales.

Business-to-consumer presentations are less complex than committee-based presentations because they are normally delivered to individuals or couples. For example, insurance agents more often than not provide presentations to individual buyers or partners. In business-to-consumer presentations, the presenter has only the needs of one or two people to focus on and can, therefore, center the presentation exclusively on their individual needs.

Although each presentation type has its own dynamics and challenges, each requires similar delivery skills and strategies that are addressed in subsequent chapters. The primary emphasis of this book will be on *business-to-business* and *business-to-consumer* presentations.

Integrity: The Foundation of Winning Sales Presentations

A young Englishman searching for the secret of success sought the advice of a wealthy businessman in London.

"Go over to the window, look out, and tell me what you see," said the businessman.

"I see the marketplace," the youth replied.

"Now go look into the mirror and tell me what you see."

"Well, naturally, I see myself."

"In each case you were looking through a pane of glass. Tell me, what's the difference?" the businessman asked.

"The window is a clear pane of glass that allows me to see out and see the people in the marketplace. The mirror has a backing of silver that reflects my image."

"Therein lies the secret of success: When you let silver come between you and the people in the marketplace, you are only going to see yourself."

Winning Sales Presentations is not a program of clever gimmicks or manipulative techniques. It is a system based on values, trust, and integrity. It is a *customer-centered* system designed to help salespeople stop thinking in terms of products and features, and start thinking in terms of buyer needs, goals, and objectives. Using the principles of *Winning Sales Presentations* salespeople develop meaningful relationships and advance buyers through the sales cycle using honest, effective presentation strategies.

Presenting with integrity is not only the right thing to do, it is the smart thing to do. Because buyers make assessments about the character and integrity of presenters, it is imperative to demonstrate honesty and integrity throughout the presentation process. Buyers need to know that presenters are trustworthy. "Am I dealing with Vinny the back slapping, plaid-jacketed, used-car salesman trying to sell me a pink Yugo, or is this someone I can trust?" As the great sales educator Zig Ziglar says, "The most important persuasion tool you have in your entire arsenal is integrity." Without integrity, salespeople severely limit their ability to establish honest rapport and build long-term relationships with clients.

Note on References

Traditional sales cycles have four steps, each step requiring a different skill set. To help sellers master each skill set, *Patrick Henry & Associates* provides training programs and books that specifically address each stage of the selling process.

	Sales Cycle	Book Title
1.	Prospecting	*Power Prospecting*
2.	Investigating	*The DNASelling Method*
3.	Presenting	*Winning Sales Presentations*
4.	Closing	*Sales-Side Negotiation*

Each book provides sales professionals and business people a comprehensive assessment of the chosen topic. Combined, the books offer sellers and managers a complete reference library that addresses each step in the selling process.[1]

Note on Format

Winning Sales Presentations is formatted by section and chapter. Each step of the sales cycle is addressed in its own section. Subsequent chapters address the specific skills and strategies associated with the appropriate stage of the sales cycle.

Where there is a need for special emphasis, one of three alert windows is used:

> **Note:** A "Note" is an idea, concept, or principle that is highlighted for clarity and impact.

> **Caution!** The "Caution" window makes sellers aware of potential presentation mistakes to avoid.

> **The Point?** "The Point" focuses the reader on the prominent principle or main idea of the section or chapter.

1. For more information about *Power Prospecting, The DNASelling Method*, and *Sales-Side Negotiation* visit www.PatrickHenryInc.com or call 1 (877) 204-4341.

Thank you for your interest in promoting and exercising *Winning Sales Presentation* strategies. I urge you to draw upon your own experiences to personalize and adapt the material to fit your own business or situation. I also encourage you to share your comments, experiences, and implementation questions regarding *Winning Sales Presentations* with *Patrick Henry & Associates.*

Best Regards.

Patrick Henry Hansen

I

part one

Pre-Presentation Preparation

1. Presentation Skills: Why They Matter
2. Preparation Precedes Power
3. Pre-Presentation Qualification
4. Pre-Presentation Needs Analysis
5. Presentation Logistics

Chapter 1

Presentation Skills: Why They Matter

All the world's a stage and all the men and women merely players.

—William Shakespeare

After the Civil War, Southern general George Pickett (famous for leading Pickett's Charge at the battle of Gettysburg) traveled to Washington D.C. for a post war interview with a prominent journalist. While traveling on a train, he listened to a conversation among a group of southerners arguing over the reasons for the Confederacy's defeat at Gettysburg. "General Lee mismanaged the situation." "Jeb Stuart ought not to have ridden off on his raid against the Union flank." "James Longstreet's lack of cooperation and vigor in the assaults of July 2nd and 3rd are to blame."

After a lengthy and heated conversation, one of the men recognized General Pickett and asked him to offer his opinion about why the South lost at Gettysburg. General Pickett replied, "I've always thought the Yankees had something to do with it."

Sometimes the most obvious answer is the most frequently overlooked answer.

While conducting presentation trainings, I am often asked, "What is the difference between a good presentation and a bad presentation," or "What is the primary factor that separates a successful presentation from an unsuccessful presentation?"

The answer is, of course, "The presenter."

Presenting: Your Most Important Selling Skill

I'll pay more for a man's ability to express himself than for any other quality he might posses.

—Charles Schwab

It's a simple fact. Regardless of your job, industry, or business, the more effective your presentations are the more successful you will be. All professions require some form of presentation. From the job interview to the corporate boardroom, every occupation necessitates some amount of presentation skill. Few professions, however, have a higher need for presentation skills than the sales profession. Sales professionals routinely deliver presentations—the outcome of which determines the level of income they will earn.

Salespeople engage in a variety of sales activities—from prospecting, to investigating, to closing. However, perhaps no sales activity has a greater impact on a sale's success or failure than a person's ability to deliver a high impact presentation. The discipline separating high earning salespeople from low earning salespeople is effective presentation skills. Even product and service capabilities are reflected in a salesperson's ability to present. More often than not, what separates one product or service from another is not features and capabilities, but the skills of the salesperson presenting the features and capabilities.

Presenting is Selling

Although selling and presenting are considered separate disciplines, in reality they are extensions of the same branch. They belong together. In fact, selling and presenting are not only compatible, they are usually inseparable.

Because of technology, increased competition, and the growing number of sellers receiving presentation training, there is a corresponding need for professional sellers to learn how to deliver exceptional presentations. It is no longer an option for sellers to neglect acquiring effective presentation skills. Many companies hire or contract with professional presenters to make high-value presentations.

> **Note:** Unprepared, untrained presenters who compete with prepared, trained competitors are at a severe disadvantage.

The Role of Skill in Presentations

How important are presentation skills in sales? How often are commissionable dollars and company profits lost by a lack of presentation skills?

In our executive retreats and corporate sales trainings I ask participants "what is the purpose of business?"[1] I get a flood of answers. "To make customers happy." "To meet the needs of the market." "To serve our clients." "To make money."

While all of these answers are partially correct, none of them hits on the true purpose of business. The answer is not complicated. In fact, it's found in a single word: profitability. The purpose of business is to increase profitability. Businesses cannot achieve any of the lofty goals and ideals noted in the previous paragraph without good, old-fashioned, Adam Smith profit.

There are three ways to increase profitability:

1. Increase Sales
2. Increase Sales Margins
3. Decrease Costs

That's it. To increase profitability you can increase sales. You can increase sales margins. You can decrease costs. Or, you can do a combination of the three. Is it possible to do all three simultaneously? Absolutely. I focus on ways to increase sales in *Power Prospecting* and *The DNASelling Method.* Increasing sales margins is discussed in *Sales-Side Negotiation.*[2]

---

1. For more information about executive retreats and corporate sales trainings contact Patrick Henry & Associates, Inc., www.PatrickHenryInc.com or call toll-free (877) 204-4341.

2. See Chapter, "The Buyer Method", in *Sales-Side Negotiation.*

Note: The most effective means of increasing sales is increasing selling and presenting skills.

The Presentation Skill Scale

Can we agree that some sales are going to be *won* regardless of the skills of a presenter? Can we agree that some sales are going to be *lost* regardless of the skills of a presenter? Can we also agree that some sales are going to be *won or lost* because of the skills of a presenter?

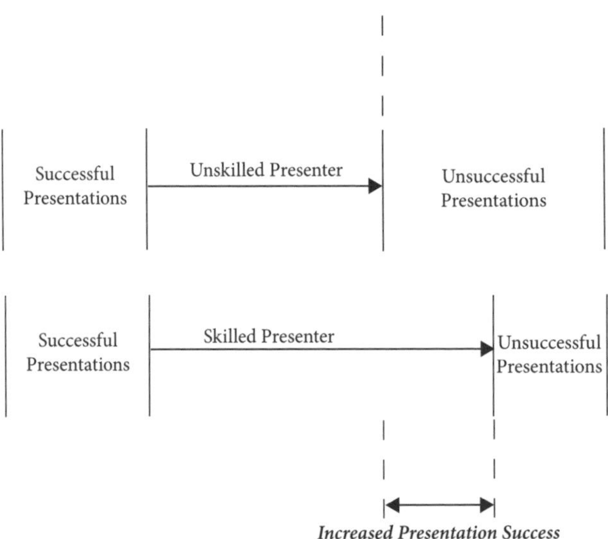

Figure 1.1

The answer, of course, to each question is "Yes." The logical conclusion is that the controlling factor of a successful presentation is skill. The skill of the presenter is the primary factor for delivering successful presentations and increasing sales performance.

Presentation skills determine the width of the middle tier of the skill scale. (See *Figure 1.1*). Skills determine the level of success a presenter experiences. Skilled presenters widen the middle tier and shrink the unsuccessful tier. The middle tier is what author Stephen R. Covey calls the "circle of influence." Because sellers can control, influence, and determine their skill level, they can directly impact their presentation success.

Presentation Skills—the Real Competitive Difference

I once arrived early at a presentation to look over the room and ensure that all of the technical capabilities were available to facilitate my presentation. When I approached the presentation room, I was in for a little shock. My main competitor was in the room making a presentation! As any cerebral salesperson would do, I sat outside the door and listened. My stomach sank as I listened to my competitor's presentation. He was smooth. He was funny. He obviously knew his product, and gauging from the audience's response, they loved his presentation. I knew I was facing a skilled competitor.

As I sat in the hall waiting for my time to present, my mind began churning over all of the competitive advantages our product offered. I began writing down a list of features and benefits unique to our product. As I continued making the list, though, it dawned on me—"It's not the product that is going to make the difference. It's the presentation."

Fortunately, I was prepared. I had been anticipating this particular presentation for quite some time. As fate would have it, I delivered one of the best presentations of my life and won the sale. That experience burned a permanent mark in my memory. Presentation skills, more often than not, are the determining factor in sales. The determining factor is not the product. It's not the features and capabilities of the product. It's not the quality of the brochures or marketing collateral, nor is it the corporate reputation. It is the seller's skill when communicating those qualities and capabilities to buyers.

Let's face it: in sales, most products and services are within a stone's throw of similarity. Yes, every product or service has certain unique characteristics and capabilities. Nonetheless, what often separates successful products from unsuccessful products is the caliber of the salespeople presenting those unique characteristics and capabilities.

In Summary

For most salespeople, presenting is the most exciting part of the sales cycle. It is also the most challenging. Delivering high impact presentations is no easy task. More than any other stage of the sales cycle, the presenting stage requires the most skill. It is also the most influential regarding the success or failure of a sale. Successful presentations lead to sales. Unsuccessful presentations lead to failure. Obviously, acquiring presentation skills is vital.

Creating and delivering a successful presentation is anything but simple. Presenters need a solid understanding of the elements of a successful presentation, a grasp of the latest presentation technologies, and a plan for creating powerful presentation content. What sales professionals need most of all, though, are real, substantive, effective presentation skills.

The Point? Whether presenting to one person or one thousand, the skill of transmitting ideas in a coherent and compelling fashion is a survival skill in the sales profession.

Chapter 2

Preparation Precedes Power

It takes three weeks to prepare a good ad-lib speech.

—Mark Twain

In 1960, John F. Kennedy stunned America by defeating the heavily favored Republican candidate, Richard Nixon, by the narrowest margin in U.S. history. His election was widely recognized as a turning point in American history that broke one of the strongest political taboos at the time—electing a Catholic in a country that considered itself a Protestant nation.

Immediately following his election, President Kennedy began drafting his inaugural address. He knew that his inaugural speech would signal the arrival of a forty-four year old president and a new generation of power in Washington. He hired Theodore Sorensen, a well-known political speechwriter, to spearhead the project. President Kennedy instructed Sorensen to study Abraham Lincoln's Gettysburg address for inspiration, content, and speech duration.

Paragraphs, pages, and complete drafts poured into the White House from noted scholars, journalists, and clergy. Biblical quotations were submitted from Billy Graham and political insight from J. K. Galbraith and Arthur Schlesinger. Still, President Kennedy was not satisfied. He wanted to deliver an epic inaugural address that would be remembered in the annals of history. He knew that traditional content, preparation, and delivery would not suffice. He insisted on draft after draft until he got what he wanted.

His dogged persistence and unprecedented preparation paid off. On January 20th, 1961, President Kennedy delivered one of the most renowned inaugural addresses in United States history.

> We observe today not a victory of party, but a cel-

ebration of freedom—celebrating an end, as well as a beginning—signifying renewal as well as change. For I have sworn before you and Almighty God the same solemn oath our forebears prescribed nearly a century and three quarters ago… Let every nation know, whether it wishes us well or ill, that we shall pay any price, bear any burden, meet any hardship, support any friend, oppose any foe, in order to ensure the survival of liberty. This we pledge and more… The energy, the faith, the devotion which we bring to this endeavor will light our country and all who serve it…

In his speech, President Kennedy announced that the torch of responsibility had passed to leaders "born in this generation." He silenced his critics by pointing out that to exclude men under the age of forty-four from positions of power and influence would have prevented Thomas Jefferson from writing the Declaration of Independence and George Washington from commanding the continental army. He also sent a firm message of resolve to the communist governments of his day.

Critics have since ranked Kennedy's address with that of Jefferson and Lincoln and credited his success, in large part, to the amount of attention and preparation he devoted to his speech.

President Kennedy knew that preparation precedes power.

Preparation: Your Key to Presentation Success

It's not a new concept that good salesmanship is 90 percent preparation and 10 percent presentation. Mental and emotional preparation equips presenters with confidence, which has a significant impact on a presentation. The prepared presenter is a competent presenter. The competent presenter is a confident presenter.

The more time presenters spend preparing, rehearsing, and practicing presentations, the more likely they are to succeed. Presenters who spend ample time preparing for a presentation feel a sense of mental certainty and emotional confidence in relation to the content and delivery of the presentation.

Note: The only way to present with confidence is to feel confident. There are no shortcuts. To feel confident, presenters need to feel mentally prepared and well versed in the topic, subject, or product being presented.

Overcoming Presentation Anxiety

The mind is a wonderful thing. It starts working the minute you are born and never stops until you get up to speak in public.

—Roscoe Drummond

Presentations are as old as history. When Moses was called on to present Jehovah's demands on the Pharaoh of Egypt, apparently he had a biblical case of stage fright. "Moses said unto the Lord, 'O my Lord, I am not eloquent, neither heretofore, nor since thou has spoken unto thy servant: but I am slow of speech and of a slow tongue'"[1]

Every presenter has lost sleep in anticipation of giving a presentation. Even the most experienced presenters sometimes experience "stage fright," "communication apprehension," or "presentation anxiety." Slight nervousness is common to presenters and should not be feared or dreaded. In fact, any presenter who does not feel at least a little pre-presentation apprehension should check his or her pulse. Many presenters actually welcome a little pre-presentation nervousness as a way of getting the "juices flowing."

However, severe nervousness is a different matter entirely. Severe nervousness can paralyze a presenter both verbally and, in a sense, physically. Obviously, severe nervousness can negatively affect the outcome of a presentation. Therefore, an important presentation skill for

1. Exodus 4:10

people who experience acute pre-presentation anxiety is taking steps to overcome nervousness.

Each presenter has his or her own method for overcoming pre-presentation nervousness. Some find that going for a brisk walk helps. Others find that lying flat on their back and engaging in deep breathing helps. I have even met presenters who find that chewing an entire pack of gum just before presenting helps them relax.

Sometimes when presenters are nervous they forget content or major points of discussion. There are two simple techniques to overcome this dilemma: preparing a presentation outline or notes to use during a presentation (see Chapter 7) or using flipcharts and writing secret inscriptions on the flipchart pages by lightly penciling in a few key words or phrases.

Caution! Inadequate preparation can lead to severe pre-presentation anxiety and affect the delivery and success of a presentation.

I have heard, read, and experienced dozens of pre-presentation relaxation methods. While all of them have some merit and can be useful, nothing beats good, old-fashioned preparedness. Adequate preparation is the best tool for defeating severe pre-presentation nervousness. Prepared presenters are typically less nervous and more confident about delivering a presentation. Though it is true that even prepared presenters experience pre-presentation anxiety, it is not the all-encompassing, paralyzing fear and nervousness that unprepared presenters feel.

The Power of Information

In early 1943, Allied forces were preparing a massive invasion of Nazi-occupied Europe. Their base of operation was North Africa, and their initial target was the island of Sicily. To diminish defense fortifications, British officers concocted a fantastic scheme of deception code named *Operation Mincemeat.*

British officers seized the corpse of a homeless man from a London morgue and gave him a completely new identity. The corpse was outfitted with a uniform and identified as Major William Martin, a military courier. A briefcase that was handcuffed to his wrist contained items that created a convincing illusion of a genuine British soldier—love letters, overdue bills, and an old bus ticket. The briefcase also contained forged documents outlining an invasion of Greece, not Sicily. British spymasters used a submarine to drop the body off the coasts of Spain, making it look as though had died in a plane crash.

As planned, Spanish authorities rushed the papers to the Germans. Hitler inspected the captured information and immediately ordered the defense of Greece to be top priority. He commissioned his most capable general, Field Marshal Erwin Rommel, to mastermind the defense.

Lacking accurate data or validated information, the Germans had been completely duped. While the German High Command was constructing defense fortifications in Greece, Allied forces, under the leadership of British general Bernard Montgomery and U.S. general George Patton, successfully invaded Sicily.

In any industry or endeavor, accurate information is of supreme importance. For this reason, professional athletic teams study film of their opponents. Countries spend huge amounts of money and take giant political and military risks to finance spies, all to gain information.

It's really not too different for a sales professional. The more information a presenter has the more power he or she wields. Information about buyer needs, pains, and problems is particularly empowering. (See Chapter 4 on conducting a pre-presentation needs-analysis). When presenters are aware of buyer needs, pains, and problems i.e., their primary buying motives—they are equipped with presentation muscle. When presenters know of dilemmas, dissatisfactions, or unresolved problems, they can use that information to emphasize specific product or service solutions. Without accurate information, presenters, like the

German High Command, make decisions based on notions, gut feelings, and faulty assumptions. I experienced the power of information when I delivered a presentation to an executive team that was evaluating my sales training program. Prior to the presentation, I researched this company's Web site to familiarize myself with the nature of their business. I identified industry specific terminology. I wrote down the corporate mission statement and used an Internet search engine to identify their main competitors. In other words, I did my homework. The information I gained from my initial research equipped me with presentation power. To start the presentation, I quoted their corporate mission statement and then linked it directly to the need for sales training. The research enabled me to use terminology and language that conveyed a familiarity with their industry. I also dropped the names of their competitors. The executive team was shocked at my knowledge of their business and industry and agreed to implement my training programs.

The information I acquired when researching and preparing my presentation content equipped me with what is called the power of CIA (Counter Intelligence & Account-information).[2] Presenters exercise the power of CIA when they attain account information and leverage it during a presentation. Like the Central Intelligence Agency of the United States government, the power of CIA rests in information. The concept of the power of CIA is captured nicely in the popular saying "Knowledge is power."

Knowledge and information are powerful presentation tools. Knowledge about an audience, a business, or market builds credibility. Be aware that the opposite is also true. Ignorance has a way of diminishing a presenter's credibility and empowering competitors.

---

2. See Chapter 8 in *Sales-Side Negotiation* for more information on the power of CIA and an in-depth analysis of the importance of building power in the selling and presenting process.

The Point? The more information presenters have about an audience, business, or industry—the more power they have to deliver a compelling presentation.

Researching Material

Winning presenters allocate sufficient time to research and explore as many information sources about their topic, business, or audience as possible.

A great starting point for conducting pre-presentation research is the Internet. The Internet can provide presenters with vast amounts of information and is the equivalent of an international, electronic library. Corporate Web sites and industry related chat rooms have reservoirs of information to familiarize presenters with industry-specific language, terminology, and verbiage to be used in presentations. Well-chosen key words can be used on search engines to find client competitors and relevant reference material.

Other sources of information include books, newspapers, trade magazines, public financial records, and professional journals.[3]

Note: Exercise the power of CIA by ordering one share of your client's stock. As a shareholder, you will receive press releases, financial and quarterly reports, and other useful "insider" information you can use in a presentation.

3. All the standard financial reports about most public companies are available free of charge on the Internet at www.FreeEdgar.com

Product Knowledge

When Bill Gates launched Microsoft, he met with IBM officials about providing an operating system for their personal computer (PC). IBM initially decided to go with 8-bit processor technology. Because of Gates' intimate knowledge of the personal computing industry, he was able to suggest major design modifications. Of course, his recommended design changes would require a new operating system—a system he agreed to provide. IBM rewarded the contract to Gates.

Why was Gates able to pull off the most lucrative deal in business history? It boils down to one factor: Bill Gates' technical knowledge. His familiarity with the technical industry allowed him to make credible recommendations that were taken seriously by the largest technology company in the world, IBM.

Whether you are selling mortgage loans, high tech software, or life insurance, adequate product or service knowledge needs to be demonstrated in a presentation. Presenters who fail to demonstrate sufficient product knowledge lose credibility and miss the opportunity to provide compelling product or service value to buyers.

It's an undeniable fact that sellers cannot present well if they do not have ample product or service knowledge. Presenters with insufficient product knowledge cannot answer fundamental product or service related questions. That situation is not only extremely embarrassing and uncomfortable for both parties, it is also unprofessional.

To avoid such a situation, winning presenters study product manuals, corporate Web sites, and marketing collateral to familiarize themselves with the features, capabilities, and benefits associated with their product or service. They do what it takes to learn and demonstrate adequate product knowledge so that they don't waste the buyer's time and undermine their presentation opportunities.

Sales Presentation Types

In the introduction, I mentioned the different types of presentations: podium, platform, business-to-business, and business-to-consumer presentations. Business-to-business and business-to-consumer presentations are the most common form of sales presentations and can be broken down into two categories:

1. Introductory Presentations
2. Solution Presentations

Each presentation addresses a different stage in the sales cycle and has a different objective (See *Figure 2.1*). In order to prepare a presentation, presenters must first determine the type of presentation being delivered.

The Introductory Presentation

The introductory presentation represents the initial contact between buyers and sellers and is used primarily to solicit interest and advance buyers to the investigation stage of the sales cycle. For example, the first few minutes of a cold call are considered an introductory presentation. The introductory presentation is provided by sellers in the opening phone or face-to-face meeting. It is less formal than solution presentations, typically conversational, and conducted in the initial few minutes of the sales conversation.

The introductory presentation informs buyers about the fundamental features and capabilities of proposed goods or services. It is a quick presentation. In fact, phone and teleprospecting presentations are usually scripted to be succinct and clear. The teleprospecting presentation highlights core features and characteristics of proposed goods or services so that buyers can quickly grasp potential capabilities and agree to advance the sale.[4]

Keep in mind that the purpose of the introductory presentation is to *introduce* capabilities, not demonstrate capabilities. Its purpose is to elicit buyer interest in product or service capabilities and to advance buyers to the investigation stage of the sales cycle, nothing more. The

---

4. For more information regarding cold calling scripts, see Chapter 10 in *Power Prospecting*.

> **Note:** The introductory presentation is quick and to the point. It's not meant to be a doctoral thesis. It's meant to be a "pre-game" show that grabs the attention and curiosity of buyers.

Solution Presentation

Once products and services have been introduced, buyers determine whether or not they see value in continuing the conversation or sale. For sellers engaged in prospecting activities, such as cold calling or attempting to set up appointments, scheduling a solution presentation is the purpose of the call.

The solution presentation is conducted after the investigation stage of the sales cycle and after the needs and problems (the primary buying motives) of buyers have been identified. The solution presentation typically (not always) occurs later in the selling process. It is used to match solutions and benefits to specific buyer needs, pains, and problems identified earlier in the sales process. *In other words, the solution presentation moves presentation content from the general to the specific.*

Because need and problem related questions equip sellers with information to match core solutions with critical client needs, solution presentations should follow need and problem related questions.[5] For that reason, solution presentations are provided after a thorough needs analysis is conducted. Without knowing the needs and problems of buyers, sellers cannot make informed recommendations or demonstrate clear and compelling benefits.

> **Note:** Benefits only apply to explicit needs. Product features and capabilities are of no value to a buyer unless they address specific needs or problems.

---

5. See Chapter 7 in *The DNASelling Method* for a detailed discussion on Need-Problem questions.

The DNASelling Map[6]

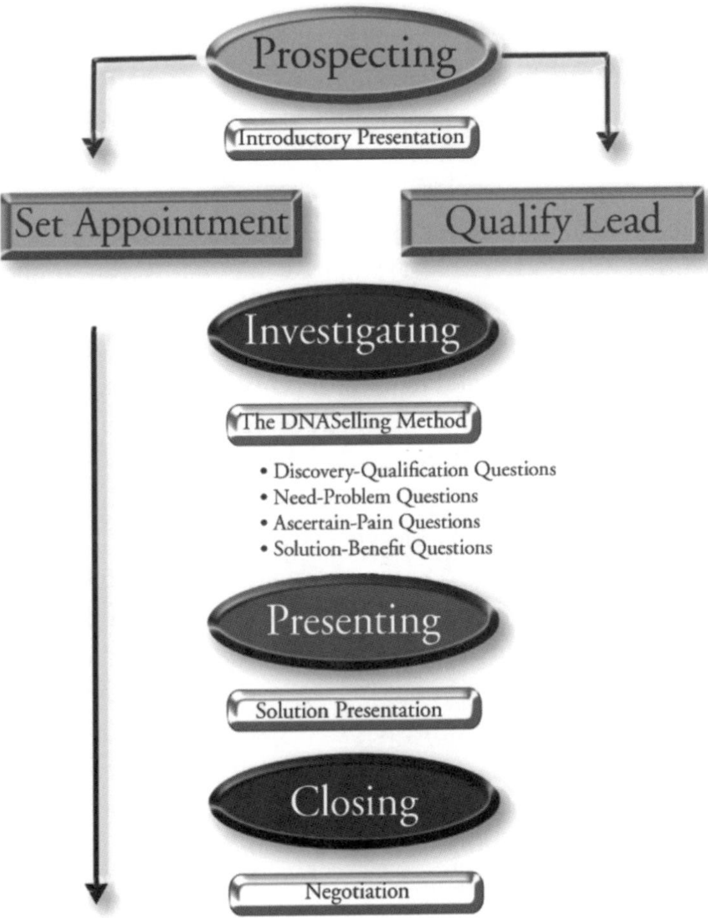

Figure 2.1

---

6. For more information regarding The DNASelling Method see, Part 2 in *The DNASelling Method*. For information regarding prospecting see *Power Prospecting*. For information regarding negotiation see, *Sales-Side Negotiation*.

Trainees frequently ask what the difference is between an introductory presentation and a solution presentation. Introductory presentations inform and educate buyers about general features and capabilities of proposed products or services and center on general product or service advantages. Solution presentations focus on matching identified needs and problems to the benefits of proposed solutions. Solution presentations are exact, not generic. They hammer exclusively on what is important and relevant to buyers.

Each presentation addresses a different stage in the sales cycle and has a different objective. For example, while selling educational software I cold called a technical coordinator for a school district in San Francisco, California. I initially used my cold calling script to gain the interest of the buyer and deliver an *introductory* presentation. After briefly describing our software, I asked a few discovery-qualification and need-problem questions. Both interested and qualified, I proceeded to provide a more detailed description of the capabilities of our software program. Seeing the potential benefits of our product, the technical coordinator invited me to deliver a presentation to his colleagues in the district. However, before I traveled to San Francisco, I called each of his colleagues. Using need-problem questions (see Chapter 4) I identified the specific needs and problems of the decision makers. Using the information I acquired in my pre-presentation phone calls, I delivered a *solution* presentation that matched our software solutions to the exact problems being experienced throughout the school district. By showing how our software program solved their specific problems, I built enormous power, circumvented my competitors, and was unanimously selected by the committee.

Note: Obviously, in many cases sellers are provided limited presentation opportunities. If necessary, it is possible to combine both presentation types—introductory and solution presentations—into one meeting.

In Summary

"Pre-presentation preparation precedes power" is a central theme at our presentation trainings. Identifying presentation types, researching audience and business subject matter, and having sufficient product or service knowledge establishes a foundation for building and delivering successful presentations.

Presentations are more appealing to buyers when it is obvious that the presenter is prepared and knowledgeable about the topic at hand. The more prepared the presenter, the higher the chances are for delivering a successful presentation. Whether the presentation is an inaugural address for the president of the United States or a presentation to a committee of technicians, adequate preparation is the key to success.

Chapter 3

Pre-Presentation Qualification

In respect of military method, we have, firstly measurements; secondly, estimation of quantity; thirdly, calculation; fourthly, balancing of chances; fifthly, victory.

—Sun-Tzu

In 1429, Jehanne D'arc (Joan of Arc) proclaimed to her French countrymen that she was on a mission from God to save France from English rule. Born a peasant, Joan began having visions in her teens about her role in liberating France. Her story is compelling. She convinced knights, local magistrates, and high officials that she had a divine mission that was imperative to the survival of France. She was eventually granted an appearance before the king.

Traveling hundreds of kilometers, she entered the king's court dressed in man's clothing and brandishing a sword. More than three hundred of the king's knights thronged the palace. Legend has it that when Joan entered the king's hall, King Charles disguised himself to see if Joan could identify him from the crowd. She did. Joan greeted the king and said that God had sent her to help him recover his country. By recognizing the king, she successfully gained the king's trust as well as his support.

Know Your Audience

Although supernatural clairvoyance isn't necessary in preparing for a presentation, recognizing, researching, and understanding your audience is.

The first law of sales presentations is *"Know your audience."* Presenters should find out as much as possible about who will be attending the presentation. Presenters should know the identity, needs, and expectations of each participant. They should know why each participant is attending. The more a presenter knows about his or her audience, the better he or she will be able to deliver a successful presentation.

Find and recognize the UDMs (Ultimate Decision Makers)—the kings and queens of the committee or decision making body.

It is important to determine the size of an audience because it impacts the way a presentation is structured. Small audiences allow plenty of opportunity for two-way interaction. Large audiences, on the other hand, require a very different approach because the communication will be almost entirely one-way. Because there is less interaction with larger audiences, it is vital that the material is clear, precise, and easy to follow.

When planning presentations, use the following checklist to identify the key characteristics of an audience:

- ❑ What is the size of the audience?
- ❑ What is the age distribution of the audience?
- ❑ Why are they attending the presentation?
- ❑ What do they expect to gain from the presentation?
- ❑ How familiar are they with the presentation topic?

Armed with the answers to these questions, presenters can prepare content and material to fit the needs, demographics, and expertise level of an audience.

Pre-Presentation Qualification

The second law of sales presentations is *"Qualify, Qualify, Qualify."* There is nothing worse than arriving to deliver a presentation only to realize that the prospective account is not qualified to purchase the good or service. Realizing that decision makers are not present, funding has been lost, decision timeframes have been pushed out, or that needs and objectives have changed *after arriving to deliver a presentation* can be avoided with pre-presentation qualification.

As a sales manager, I attended a software presentation with a sales representative in San Diego, California. The salesperson was excited about the size of the potential sale and asked me to attend. The presentation went well and the attendees seemed impressed with our product. I sensed a lack of urgency, however, on the committee's part to implement our solution. At the conclusion of the presentation, I asked the committee a simple qualifying question, "What timeframe are you looking at to implement this project?" They answered, "Sometime later next year." My colleague was shocked and later embarrassed. Although this company was interested in the product, their timeframe to implement the project was over a year away. No budget had been assigned, and the ultimate decision makers were not in the room. In other words, the entire presentation had been a complete waste of time, money, and effort on our part. My colleague gave an excellent presentation, but it was of no value. Although the attendees liked what they saw, they would have to repeat the evaluation process once the budget and timeframe were firmly established. Had that simple timeframe question been asked prior to the presentation, we would have saved ourselves time, money, and effort—all of which could have been invested elsewhere.

> **Note:** Winning presenters pre-qualify accounts prior to investing significant amounts of time and effort preparing presentations, traveling to client locations, and delivering solution presentations.

I worked with a CEO who casually made the statement, "Everything in life is a trade off." Although initially I didn't think much about his statement, later that evening I pondered over the profundity of his words. Regardless of what you are doing, you could be doing something else. If a person chooses to watch a sitcom, he is trading it off for reading a book, going for a jog, or spending time with his family. Everything we do is a trade-off. Since that time, I have been extremely careful what I "trade off" in life.

In the sales arena, spending time and effort on one client means you are trading it off for another. The key is to spend time and effort on clients with the greatest purchasing potential.

The Point? Focus on high probability buyers, not unqualified prospects.

The DNASelling Method

On February 28, 1953, Francis Crick walked into the Eagle pub in Cambridge, England, and announced that he and James Watson had "found the secret of life." In just a few weeks of frenzied inspiration, the two men made one of the most profound discoveries in history. They built a model of deoxyribonucleic acid (DNA) that demonstrated how the very structure of DNA provided one of life's most essential features: the storage and transmission of genetic code. They solved a problem that had baffled the scientific community for years—how did the DNA molecule make exact copies of itself? Biochemists already knew that DNA contained a biological code, a genetic language that consisted of four types of molecules known as bases—adenine, cytosine, guanine, and thymine—referred to as A, C, G, and T. How those molecules made exact replicas of each other was still a mystery.

Back in the Cavendish Laboratory in Cambridge, Watson and Crick concentrated on identifying the *form* of DNA rather than its *function*. They built model after model of the possible structure of DNA until on March 7, 1953, they discovered their solution. They found that DNA is a double helix shaped like a spiral staircase with the four bases representing the steps. Their model suggested a mechanism by which DNA could make copies of itself. The two strands of genes that make up the DNA molecule can simply unzip or unravel into reverse images of each other that can act as templates for new strands to build on.

As Watson and Crick discovered, the genius of DNA is that *its form is its function*. Its shockingly simplistic double helix structure allows the molecules to make facsimiles of itself. Because the bases always bond in the exact sequence, the finished copies are always the same. The concept was stunning in its implications.

Using the scientific method, Watson and Crick made the most celebrated discovery of the twentieth century. The double helix now stands as an icon of the scientific understanding of life.

Using an Effective Questioning Methodology

Like most sales professionals, I discovered early in my career that selling is more of a science than an art. I learned that asking the right questions is more important than looking for the right answers. Still, knowing how important it was to ask the right questions was not enough. My questions seemed random, at times even uncomfortable. Asking questions "off the top of my head" was sporadic and ineffective. This unorganized approach quite often left me tongue-tied and unable to communicate effectively. I needed a system—a questioning methodology. I needed a process that was easy to understand, easy to remember, and easy to replicate from one sale to the next. I decided to write down a series of questions that I deemed important to making sales. I then organized the questions into categories. For example, I separated qualification questions from questions that identified client needs. I differentiated need related questions from solution related questions. The result was *The DNASelling Method*—a questioning methodology that leads buyers through the sales cycle.

The same way DNA consists of the building blocks of life, *The DNASelling Method* consists of the building blocks of effective selling. Similar in concept to DNA, *The DNASelling Method* is a selling language—a code of questions. It is a process of discovery—a questioning framework whose "form is its function."

The DNASelling Method is a question-based approach to selling that follows a rational probing sequence. This sequence provides sellers with a systematic approach to qualifying accounts and closing sales. Like the four bases of DNA, *The DNASelling Method* consists of four probing categories that guide buyers and sellers through the purchasing process:[1]

D **Discovery-Qualification Questions**: questions that discover a buyer's existing circumstance, account facts, qualification factors, and purchasing capabilities.

N **Need-Problem Questions:** questions that identify a buyer's needs, problems, and primary buying motives.

A **Ascertain-Pain Questions**: questions that ascertain the negative consequences of unfulfilled needs and/or unresolved problems, i.e., the pain.

S **Solution-Benefit Questions**: questions that focus on the benefits of implementing the proposed solution.

Because questioning is such a fundamental part of successful selling, it's important to use an effective questioning methodology—a strategy. By using *The DNASelling Method*, sellers identify decision makers prior to making presentations, and add structure, repeatability, and predictability to the presenting process.[2]

> **Note:** *The DNASelling Method* is a dialogue for asking questions—not a rigid formula. It is a map, a guideline, and framework that is flexible and adaptable. It is not a strict or inflexible sales algorithm.

1. To learn how to implement *The DNASelling Method* in your business or sales situation, contact *Patrick Henry & Associates, Inc.* at 1 (877) 204-4341 or visit www.PatrickHenryInc.com.
2. For a comprehensive analysis of *The DNASelling Method*, see Part 2 in *The DNASelling Method.*

Discovery-Qualification Questions

A wise man doesn't give the right answers, he poses the right questions.

—Claude Levi-Strauss

Good scientists do not worry about getting the right answers. They concentrate on asking the right questions. They make intelligent inquiries, take notes, make observations, and listen. They initially gather information—they don't provide it. Likewise, great sellers do not initially focus on providing information. They focus on acquiring it.

Discovery questions are probes that focus on a prospect's existing circumstance and discover account facts, background information, and fundamental issues related to the sale. For example, a salesperson selling vehicles might ask discovery questions such as, "Mr. Jones, are you looking for trucks or vans for your delivery business?" "Are your current delivery vehicles two or four wheel drive?" A salesperson selling networking solutions should ask discovery questions to determine what networking platform the prospect is using. "Ms. Prospect, what platform are you currently using, Microsoft or Novell?" "What version of Novell are you using to run your servers?" Discovery questions not only reveal insightful information, sometimes they expose certain biases prospects have. For instance, a simple discovery question might reveal that a prospect is a Novell fanatic and hates Microsoft networking solutions.

I managed a salesperson who continually neglected to ask simple discovery questions. He seemed to view them as a waste of time and instead preferred to jump to the presentation stage of the sales cycle. He once made a sale that illustrates the importance of asking discovery questions.

The technical administrator who made the purchase called to inform me that he was returning our software a few weeks after purchasing a complete software and networking solution. I was stunned. This was a big sale, and I was completely unaware of any problems or mishaps. I asked the buyer why he wanted to return our product. He told me that he felt that our salespeople were dishonest and that he did not want to deal with a company that took advantage of its customers. When I asked him why he felt that way, he stated, "Because your sales rep sold us a Web-based product knowing that we did not yet have the hardware or networking infrastructure in place to use it!"

When I approached our salesperson to find out what happened, he was shocked to find out that they did not have the hardware or networking capability to use our Web client. He just assumed they had the technical requirements to implement our Web-based line of products. Because he failed to ask simple discovery questions that would have identified their exact technical capabilities, he sold them a solution they couldn't use.

The Point? Equipped with information that identifies a buyer's existing circumstance and account facts, sellers make better recommendations, deliver account-specific presentations, and close more sales.

Question Rationale

In 1582, Protestants in the Netherlands were struggling to gain independence from their Catholic ruler, Spain. Brutal executions and cruel torturing techniques rallied the Dutch Protestants to revolt. Seeking assistance from England, the Protestant rebels appealed to Queen Elizabeth I. Not wishing to engage in open warfare with Spain, the most powerful empire in the world at the time, Elizabeth resisted intervention. By 1585, however, she assented to a treaty which bound her to send an army to assist the Dutch Protestants. Before committing English troops, though, she issued an extraordinary twenty-page pamphlet, translated it into French, Spanish, and Dutch, and distributed it across England and the Continent. This was an unprecedented move—a sovereign ruler justifying her actions before the

The DNASelling Method

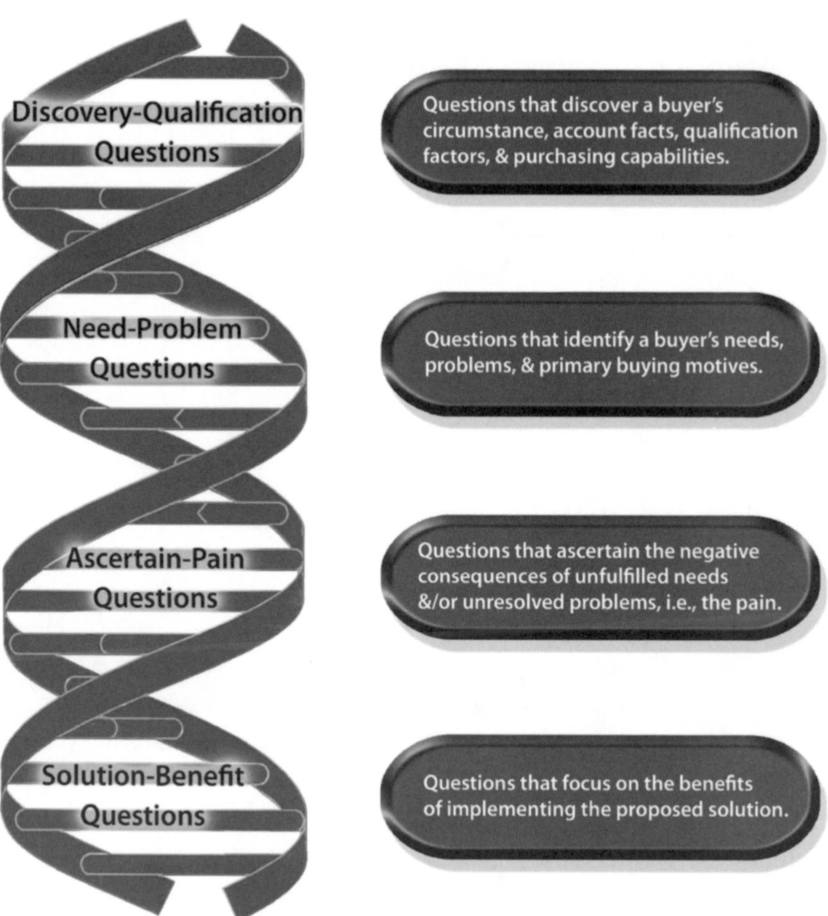

Figure 3.1

opinions of the world. In her political treatise, she provided the reason and rationale for her intervention. She discussed the tyrannical nature of Spanish governors and outlined the violation of "ancient laws of liberty." The pamphlet had the desired effect and rallied Protestants across Europe to support her decision.

Although salespeople should never feel obliged to apologize for their questions, like Queen Elizabeth I, they should be prepared to provide rationale to justify their inquiries.

When you were a kid, remember how much you feared your neighbors' big dog? When you hit a ball over the fence and had to retrieve it, how did you speak to the dog? More than likely, you approached the dog saying, "Nice doggy. Easy boy. Good dog." Why? Because you didn't want your tone to arouse the hostility of the dog. Rationale statements do the same thing. They remove the potential harshness of the question or approach.

Prospects should not feel like they are being grilled with unnecessary, useless, or endless questions. This is why cerebral sellers "tee up" their questions with a statement of rationale. The statement of rationale softens the probe and justifies the question.

For each questioning category in *The DNASelling Method*, a statement of rationale is provided prior to the sample question.

Sample *Discovery* Questions

Rationale: "Mr. Prospect, I would like to tell you about [name of your product or service]; however, in order for me to do the best job I possibly can for you, I need to ask you a few questions about how you are currently [managing X]."

Tell me more about _____.
What are you using at present to _____?
Help me understand how you currently _____.

Tell me a little bit about _____.
How many _____?
How long have you been using _____?
Tell me how you presently _____.
How many people utilize _____?

Caution! Asking too many discovery questions can bore buyers. Sellers should ask as few discovery questions as possible without missing critical account information.

Successful presenters recognize that large sales are a compilation of small sales. By following *The DNASelling Method*, sales professionals experience a series of small successes early in the sale that eventually lead to the final purchase. *The DNASelling Method* helps sellers focus on asking questions, acquiring information, and qualifying accounts—prior to the presentation.

Discovery-qualification questions are great pre-presentation tools and are critical to a presenter's success. They help sellers determine whether or not a lead is worth pursuing and if TIME (Time, Investment, Money & Effort) should be spent setting up and delivering a presentation in the first place.

Qualification Questions

Has this ever happened to you? You contact a prospect, gain his or her attention, present your product, answer questions, and prepare a proposal. You send a follow-up letter, leave messages, and finally talk to the prospect about a few specific issues. You call back a week later, and he or she tells you, "Your presentation was excellent, but I talked to my boss and he just isn't interested."

What happened? What went wrong?

Obviously, the account was not properly qualified. Had the account been qualified, the ultimate decision maker (the boss) would have attended the presentation.

Picking winnable battles is a trademark of successful sellers. Even sellers with polished communication skills, incredible product knowledge, and powerful personalities cannot be successful unless they concentrate on prospects with the greatest purchasing potential.

Sales success depends on a seller's ability to qualify leads and gain account information critical to winning a sale *prior to the presentation.* There are many interested people who will never buy. The level of buyer interest is meaningless without the ability or willingness to purchase the proposed good or service. This is why qualifying is so critical to successful selling—it helps sellers make better time investment decisions.

Qualification Characteristics

The DNASelling Method provides sellers with an organized procedure to analyze each selling opportunity systematically. Salespeople can then avoid the mistake of pursuing every prospect with the same tenacity. The objective of selling is to spend time with prospects who need, want, and *can* purchase products and services. By implementing *The DNASelling Method*, sellers use a proven system of opportunity evaluation—an objective qualification process that allows sellers to allocate time efficiently and deal with accounts that have the highest probability for success.

While selling educational software, I received a call from a prospect interested in our product. The prospect asked me to fill out a lengthy RFP (request for proposal). I invested an enormous amount of time filling out the RFP. After it was completed, I submitted the RFP to my contact person and casually asked, "So, what's the timeframe on this project?" She replied, "Well, we are hoping to get a grant from the government in early spring." My heart sank as I realized what had just happened. This prospect used me to gain information to assist their efforts in acquiring a government grant that they would then *possibly* use to purchase my product. I could not believe I had been so stupid. That experience burned a permanent reminder in my mind to never, ever invest TIME on a prospect who is not thoroughly qualified.

A qualified prospect in any industry has four general characteristics:

1. Ultimate Decision-maker(s)
2. Available Funding
3. Acceptable Timeframe(s)
4. Matching Needs

If any one of the qualifying components is missing, the probability of closing the sale is diminished. By asking simple qualification questions, sellers identify all four qualifying characteristics and enhance the probability of working with clients who are likely to purchase.

Because some leads are temptations disguised as opportunities, it's important to use a systematic approach to qualify contacts. Without a consistent process for qualifying buyers, sellers lose valuable time they might have otherwise used to pursue genuine opportunities.

The Point? You can't sell to someone who can't buy. Be sure to qualify accounts before investing significant amounts of TIME (Time, Investment, Money & Effort) into the sale.

Opinion Makers vs. Opinion Takers

The qualification step that has the greatest impact on a presentation is identifying ultimate decision makers. In the presentation stage of the sales cycle, it is imperative to confirm the attendance of people who can make decisions. Ensuring that decision makers are present provides presenters with an opportunity to match the critical needs of known decision-drivers with unique product or service solutions.

When making group or committee-based presentations, presenters should identify the *primary* decision makers. Every committee has "opinion makers" and "opinion takers." By identifying the leaders on a committee, presenters can cater to the needs and interests of the committee members who are going to have the greatest influence on the decision making process.

When conducting pre-presentation interviews, be sure to determine the position or influence of the person disseminating the information to you. Where does he or she belong in the organization? What is his or her role? How much power does he or she have?

> **Note:** Confirming the attendance of decision makers shortens the sales cycle, prevents sellers from needlessly making multiple presentations, and increases the likelihood of a favorable decision.

I delivered a presentation to a committee of technicians in Kenai, Alaska. Initially, I worked almost exclusively with a particular committee member to acquire technical and account information. He supplied me with the information I needed to understand the technical specifications and dynamics associated with the account. I developed an excellent relationship with this person and things were looking great. Then he dropped the bomb. He was not a primary decision maker on the committee. Just days before the presentation to the committee, I realized that I had been dealing with a competent technician, but a technician who, nevertheless, had no power. My primary competitor did not make the same mistake. He had latched onto the committee's most forceful personality. I immediately switched gears and began communicating directly with some of the other "opinion makers" on the decision making body.

Fortunately, my adjustment paid off, and I won the sale. I also learned a valuable lesson. *Qualify not just the account, but your point of contact as well.* Ensure that you are working with people who can both make and influence a decision. Don't get married to specific account players simply because they are willing to spend time with you. Carefully select where you are going to invest time, and with whom. If possible, make this decision prior to your presentation.

The key is to recognize primary decision makers as early as possible. Once decision makers are identified, skilled presenters then cultivate those decision makers into product champions to promote their product or service to other committee members.

The Point? Focus the bulk of your qualifying efforts on decision makers with purchasing authority and financial clout.

Creating Question Sheets

When I first started my sales career, I learned that relying solely on memory to come up with good qualifying questions was naïve. So, I created *question sheets* to assure that I would ask good questions. I printed the question sheets, put them in paper protectors, placed them on my desk, and referenced them during my calls. It was extremely effective. It systematized my qualifying efforts and was the beginning of *The DNASelling Method*.

By creating question sheets I essentially built a library of questions to reference during the investigation stage of the selling process. The following sample qualification questions are taken from those initial sheets.

Sample *Decision-Maker* Qualification Questions

Rationale: "Mr. Prospect, based on our experience in the X market, there are usually many people involved in making purchasing decisions."

> Who, other than yourself, will be involved in making the final decision?
>
> A system like ______ usually affects people at several levels of an organization. Who else is involved in the decision making process?
>
> Is there anyone else you usually consult with when making decisions of this type?
>
> Aside from yourself, who will be involved in the decision making process?

Is there anyone else who needs to be involved in order to make a decision?

> **Caution!** Do not ask questions that insinuate the person you are speaking with is not a decision-maker.

Remember, not everyone can pull the trigger and make a decision, but many people can pull the plug on your opportunity to sell. The bulk of your time should be spent with people who can put decision ink on paper. Be sure to deal with decision makers.

Sample *Funding* Qualification Questions

Rationale: "Ms. Prospect, implementation of a project like this usually depends on available funding."

How do you normally fund a project like this?

If you did choose to _____, is funding available to implement?

[ABC Product] can cost anywhere between X and Y dollars depending on what you want to accomplish. How are you planning to fund this project?

Depending on your specific needs, [automated systems] range between X and Y dollars. What does your budget look like for this project?

This particular model requires an initial investment of X dollars, and a monthly investment of Y. Is that an acceptable investment range?

What kind of a budget are you working with?

Assuming there is a fit between the problems you are experiencing and what I'm offering, the investment is going to run between X and Y dollars. Has funding been allocated for this project?

Asking funding related questions prevents finances from becoming a barrier later in the selling process. By dealing with money issues up front, cerebral sellers defuse the "we can't afford it" objection before it turns up.

Sample *Timeframe* Qualification Questions

Rationale: "Mr. Prospect, implementation of a project like this usually depends on available funding. What sort of timeframe are you working with?"

> **Note:** Used appropriately, the sample timeframe rationale question will answer both funding and timeframe issues.

Are you working with any decision deadlines?

How is the purchase decision being made?

How soon do you plan on making the decision?

As you look at implementing a _____, what kind of timeframe are you working with?

Will it be possible for you to purchase in the present budget cycle?

What decision making process do you go through when deciding on a purchase such as this?

When do you see yourself moving forward with this project?

If you decided to go forward, when would you want to start?

Thank you for telling me the timeframe. How does the decision timeframe relate to the implementation date?

Cerebral sellers match time and effort with appropriate buying cycles and implementation dates. They discover real timeframes and adjust their selling efforts accordingly.

Matching Needs

The final qualifying factor in any sale is matching needs. In order for a lead to be considered qualified, product or service capabilities must match client needs. Problems, pains, and dissatisfactions need to correspond to potential product offerings and service solutions.

In order to maximize the impact of a presentation, the needs and interests of attendees must be clearly understood. By understanding and verifying account objectives, presenters can match known needs with their product or service.

When to Qualify Leads

Although qualifying opportunities is a fundamental part of successful selling, sellers should not try to qualify the account in the first few minutes of the initial sales call.

I traveled to Cancun, Mexico, to conduct sales training for a group of franchise owners at their annual, corporate retreat. Part of the training focused on qualifying accounts. As part of our ongoing coaching program, I worked with a very intense franchise owner who seemed to understand the letter of the law but failed to understand the spirit of the law. He implemented our training on qualification and began qualifying accounts. There was just one problem. He qualified his accounts in the immediate moments of his sales calls. Because dealing with people who could not purchase his product just did not make sense to him, he decided to immediately qualify his contacts. It didn't work. He didn't "warm up" his calls with friendly conversation. He failed to put buyers at ease and neglected to discover account information. He just jumped right into qualifying the candidate, and it backfired. People felt like they were getting bashed with questions. He became an overzealous seller rather than a cerebral seller.

There Are Exceptions

Although qualifying is an elemental part of selling, in some cases it makes sense for a seller to make a presentation to an account that is not yet qualified.

After making the above statement, a sales training participant who sells high-end networking solutions asked, "Why on Earth would a salesperson set up a presentation with an account that's not qualified?" Seems like an obvious question. However, in some cases selling can be counter-intuitive. For some sellers, it makes sense to set up presentations with prospects who are not yet qualified. Why? Because the cost of the appointment is low and the potential payoff is high. Sometimes qualifying an account during the presentation (versus prior to the presentation) increases the probability for the sale.

A close friend of mine sells mortuary services. He actually sells people a complete plan for death. He sets up a financial plan to pay for the casket, the mortuary costs, the funeral expenses, the plot, everything. This prevents people from passing on financial burdens when they die. It's actually quite a responsible thing to do. When he contacts people, his sole objective is to set up a presentation. He doesn't even bother attempting to qualify them prior to the presentation. And who could blame him? Could you imagine the questions he would need to ask in order to qualify an account prior to setting up an appointment? "Hi Ms. Jones, this is Bob from Fred's Mortuary. We were wondering if anyone in your family is preparing to die. (Response)... And is Mr. Jones going to die soon as well? (Response)... Good. Were you planning on selecting caskets together or separately? (Response). And how do you normally fund purchasing things like caskets and burial plots?"

Insurance agents, business consultants, and financial planners are examples of sales professionals who set up presentations without first qualifying accounts.

In Summary

Moral victories don't count.

—Herb Kelleher,
CEO Southwest Airlines

Presenters who pre-qualify presentation participants greatly enhance the likelihood of delivering successful presentations. By qualifying accounts prior to a presentation, sellers ensure that they maximize their presentation opportunities and present to people who have the ability to buy.

Chapter 4

Pre-Presenation Needs Analysis

Seek first to understand, then to be understood

—Stephen R. Covey

In 58 B.C., a daring and arrogant Germanic tribal leader named Ariovistus openly challenged Julius Caesar and the invading Roman legions. Mindful that it would be a serious matter to make war on the Germans, Caesar sent messengers to the German leader asking for a conference. Ariovistus refused. Instead, he invited Caesar to attack, adding that no one had ever fought him without being destroyed. Caesar lost no time in taking up the challenge and marched his six legions (around thirty thousand men) at top speed to secure Vesontio, a fortified town with terrain that provided strategic military advantages.

While waiting at Vesontio for supplies, Caesar's troops mingled with the local Celtic merchants. Anxious to learn about their enemy, they questioned the townspeople about their German enemies. What they heard shocked them.

The Gaulish townspeople described tales about the physical size and fighting ferocity of the Germans. They told of their "enormous stature, incredible courage, and splendid military training."[1] The Celts claimed the Germans were a warrior race, unconquerable in battle—that when they fought them they had not even been able to bear the expressions on their faces or the fierce glance of their eyes.

Caesar's troops were seized with panic.

Caesar assembled his centurions and sent them into the ranks of his army to conduct an internal reconnaissance to determine the will and mood of his men. What he found was unsettling. His leaders reported to him that his auxiliary troops were begging for permission to leave. Wills were

1. Julius Caesar, *The Conquest of Gaul* (New York: Penguin Books, 1982) 47.

being written and questions were raised about the extraordinary military training of the Germans. Apparently the alarm was so widespread that even Caesar's tribunes were begging to depart.

Based on the information reported by the centurions, and the apparent pre-battle fear and anxiety of his troops, Caesar decided to address the issue head on. He knew that without strengthening the will of his men, the battle would be lost before it began.

Caesar assembled his army and delivered one of the most prized military speeches of all time.

> Our countrymen faced this enemy in our father's time, when Gaius Marius won a victory over the Cimbri and Teutoni, by which the whole army earned as much glory as their commander. They faced them again more recently in Italy when they defeated the rebellious slaves... This shows what a great advantage resolute courage is... If anyone is alarmed by the fact that the Germans have defeated the Gauls and put them to flight, he should inquire into the circumstances of that defeat. He will find that it happened at a time when the Gauls were exhausted by a long war... We will move camp in the early hours of the morning so as to find out with the least possible delay whether [the troops'] sense of honor and duty or their fear is stronger. If no one else will follow, I will go accompanied only by the 10th legion. Of their loyalty, I have no doubt.

His address had the desired effect and inspired his men to the utmost enthusiasm for battle. His speech transformed the disposition of his troops from fearful to fearless.

Although Ariovistus and his men fought bravely, the legionnaires made short work of the Germans and defeated them in a brutal, but victorious battle.

Need-based Presentations

Caesar's pivotal address was not some haphazard speech delivered "off the top of his head." It was an informed, well timed, and purposeful speech based on the specific fears and concerns of his troops. He based his remarks not only on the information acquired from his centurions, but also from information gained through espionage conducted in the camps of his enemy. His analysis empowered him with the information he needed to inspire the resolve and courage of his men.

Like Caesar's inspiring address to his troops, successful sales presentations are based on the specific needs, concerns, and interests of buyers. Conducting a thorough needs-analysis is the first step to achieving that objective.

Diagnostic Selling

If you visit an eye doctor and tell her that you have blurred vision, how much confidence will you have in her prognosis if she takes off her glasses and says, "Here, try these, they work for me."? Likewise, buyers will not have confidence in recommendations that are not based on an analysis of their specific needs.

In the mid 1930's, Dale Carnegie wrote,

> I go fishing up in Maine every summer. Personally, I am very fond of strawberries and cream, but I find that for some strange reason, fish prefer worms. So when I go fishing, I don't think about what I want. I think about what they want. I don't bait the hook with strawberries and cream. I dangle a worm or a grasshopper in front of the fish and say, "Wouldn't you like to have that?"

Effective sales strategies are based on needs and issues important to buyers, which is why cerebral sellers "diagnose before they prescribe." They identify what is important to the buyer so that their efforts can be focused on the prospect's *primary buying motives* (PBM). When sellers cater to the interests of the buyer, product solutions not only become more obvious, they become more urgent.

At our executive retreats and corporate trainings, I frequently ask participants, "Why should I, or anyone else, purchase your product or service?" The traditional responses are "quality," "service," "value," and "price." Unfortunately, most sellers are under the mistaken impression that quality, service, value, and price are the reasons for purchasing their products or services. The reason people purchase products and services is to solve problems. Without a need to fill or a problem to solve, quality, service, value, and price have no meaning. This is why identifying a buyer's needs and problems is so critical—it is the reason for the purchase.

Avoiding "Show up, Throw up" Sales Presentations

Remember not only to say the right thing in the right place, but far more difficult still, to leave unsaid the wrong thing at the tempting moment.

—Benjamin Franklin

During World War II, the British Intelligence agency assembled Britain's finest mathematicians and chess players to crack the German communication code. These mathematical and mechanical geniuses deciphered a predecessor to the modern computer, a machine called *Enigma*. The first intelligence Enigma deciphered was information concerning a massive bombing of Coventry, England. British Intelligence was suddenly placed in a precarious dilemma. If they scrambled extra forces to meet the attack, it would alert the Germans to the fact that their code had been broken. On the other hand, if the British did not muster a defense, thousands of people in Coventry would be killed. Winston Churchill and other British leaders decided that to achieve long term military objectives, it was necessary to allow the attack to proceed unimpeded. British leadership was forced to exercise almost unbearable patience as they watched in frustration as the town of Coventry was bombarded into rubble.

Like British military leaders during World War II, highly successful salespeople do not sacrifice long term objectives for short term advantages. They avoid the temptation to rush in and share all the information they possess about the benefits and capabilities of their product or service. Cerebral sellers exercise restraint by controlling the instinct to immediately immerse buyers with product information.

When I stepped out of corporate America to start my sales consultation business, I walked away from a premiere health insurance package. I shopped around for a good health insurance program and invited multiple insurance agents to my office for evaluation. One of the agents showed up to deliver a presentation and immediately began telling me about all of the different features of his insurance program. For close to thirty minutes, he rattled off the various programs his company offered and explained to me why they were so terrific. In other words, he delivered a traditional "show up, throw up" presentation. He did not ask a single discovery question to identify why I was looking for health insurance. He did not ask a single need or problem related question to find out what my needs were. He just bombarded me with feature after feature hoping that a few of them might "stick."

After the presentation, he asked me what I did for a living. I told him that I was a sales, negotiation, and presentation trainer. He grinned and in an almost arrogant tone asked, "So how did I do?" I replied, "Do you really want to know or are you just looking for me to slap you on the back?" He said, "No, I would really like to know." He was shocked at my response. I told him that I thought it was one of the worst presentations I had ever seen. I then discussed with him why.

Although there were multiple reasons for his poor performance, the primary mistake he made was not identifying my *primary buy-*

ing motives. He didn't even attempt to evaluate my current situation, needs, or pains, or the problems that his program could solve. Instead, he delivered what is referred to as a "ready, fire, aim" or "shotgun" sales presentation—a "feature dump." By failing to identify my critical needs, he could not focus his presentation on how his program could benefit me, my family, and my employees.

What this insurance agent should have done was ask a few discovery and need-problem related questions before making his presentation. For example, he might have asked:

> "Mr. Hansen, in order for me to focus this presentation on what matters most to you, help me understand why you are currently looking for health insurance?" (Discovery question)
>
> "As you look at health insurance programs, what are your most critical needs?" (Need question)
>
> "Are there any problems you have experienced with your previous health insurance program that you would like to avoid with a new plan?" (Problem question)

Based on the answers to these questions, this agent would have been equipped with the information he needed to focus his presentation on the *benefits* of his health insurance program (product capabilities that meet specified needs expressed by buyers) rather than the *features* of his health insurance program (product facts and characteristics). By asking a few preliminary questions, he could have avoided delivering a "spray and pray" sales presentation.

A shopper searching for kitchen knives in the house wares department of a retail store asked a salesperson "Are these kitchen knives sharp?" The salesperson answered, "Oh yes. They have been honed with laser technology. They cut deeply, leaving no rough edge." The shopper replied, "Oh. My mother loves to cook but has arthritis. I'd be afraid she would get a nasty cut."

The intent of the shopper's question was not to gain information about the technology of the knives. The intent was to introduce the issue of safety. Before rushing in with an answer a cerebral salesperson would have asked, "Are sharp knives important to you?"

The temptation is strong for undisciplined sellers to explain selling points to potential buyers prematurely. In the beginning of the sales interview, and especially prior to conducting an in-depth needs analysis, refrain from explaining what your product or service will do and concentrate on determining what your prospect needs.

> **The Point?** *The DNASelling Method* is a cure for a fundamental selling disease—jumping in too soon with a premature presentation without knowing a buyer's needs, i.e., "throwing up."

Pre-Presentation Need-Problem Questions

If you can learn a simple trick you'll get along a lot better with all kinds of folks. You never really understand a person until you consider things from his point of view… until you climb into his skin and walk around in it.

—Atticus Finch to his daughter, Scout, in, *To Kill a Mockingbird*

Like a verbal detective, the tools of the trade for cerebral sellers are questions. Questions demonstrate concern for a prospect's needs and place the focus of the sales process where it belongs: on the prospect. As the great sales educator, Zig Ziglar, stated, sellers should always "Lead with need."

The second step of the cerebral sales cycle is the investigation stage, not the presentation stage. Unfortunately, most salespeople instinctively jump from prospecting to presenting and miss the most vital step in the selling process—investigating. The investigation stage of the sales cycle provides sellers with an opportunity to gather information, identify needs, and determine prospective problems to match with product solutions.

No selling skill has greater impact on the success or failure of a sale than the ability of a seller to identify a prospective buyer's needs, problems, and pains. That bears repeating. ***Nothing you do in the selling process is more important than discovering needs, identifying problems, and determining the primary buying motives of buyers.***

> **Note:** A needs analysis is much more than just a discovery process. The competitive battle is often won in the investigation stage of the sales cycle *before* the sales presentation even takes place.

Review *The DNASelling Method*:

- **D**iscovery-Qualification Questions
- **N**eed-Problem Questions
- **A**scertain-Pain Questions
- **S**olution-Benefit Questions

The second step of *The DNASelling Method* is asking need-problem questions. Need-problem questions dig for "buzz issues," "hot buttons," and identify issues and topics that can be used to create high impact presentations and fuel the sales process.

Using need-related information, sales professionals equip themselves with the required data to make account specific, credible recommendations. *Without* need-related information, sales professionals cannot sell to needs. Without identifying needs to fill or problems to solve, there is probably no basis for a presentation in the first place.

Need-problem questions form the foundation of a successful sale and supply sellers with three essential benefits:

1. Determining whether or not there is a "good fit" between problems and solutions
2. Identifying the prospect's primary buying motives
3. Building credibility and rapport with buyers

The results are precise and accurate recommendations that buyers take seriously. Sellers who unearth buyer needs and problems and then incorporate them into sales presentations become respected consultants instead of product pushers. As Stephen R. Covey puts it, "When you can present your own ideas clearly, specifically, visually, and most important, contextually—in the context of a deep understanding of [a buyer's] paradigms and concerns—you significantly increase the credibility of your ideas... You're not wrapped up in your 'own thing,' delivering grandiose rhetoric from a soapbox."[2]

Need-problem questions help sales professionals sell with greater accuracy and greater integrity. Equipped with information about the needs, problems, difficulties, and dissatisfactions of buyers, sellers are better prepared to make substantive recommendations and meaningful presentations.

There is an additional benefit to using need-problem questions. The *process* of identifying the needs has a positive affect on the psyche of buyers. When presenters provide buyers with an opportunity to participate in defining the problems that need to be addressed, they develop a sense of ownership in the presentation and are more easily persuaded to purchase the solution.

> **The Point?** Presenters should tailor presentations to the specific needs of buyers. If they do not, they are simply animated advertising mediums rather than effective sales professionals.

Sample *Need-Problem* Questions

Rationale: "Mr. Prospect, as a [business] consultant for [*Patrick Henry & Associates*], it's my job to understand and analyze any current needs you face with regard to [sales performance] and then do my best to come up with solutions to address those problems."

2. Stephen R. Covey, *The 7 Habits of Highly Effective People* (New York: Simon and Schuster, 1989) 257.

Sample Need Questions

As you look at this project, what are your most critical needs?

What's the most significant issue you currently face?

What is it you're looking for in a _____?

As you look at _____, what capabilities are most critical to you?

What would you like to accomplish with _____?

What benefits are you most interested in when evaluating _____?

What is the most important factor for you in making this decision?

What else would help me understand _____?

What would help you do your job better?

What are three things you would like to see improved?

Sample Problem Questions

What are the most important problems you would like to resolve?

What problems are you currently experiencing?

What are the most critical challenges you currently face?

Help me understand what area is giving you the most difficulty.

What created these problems?

Are you experiencing any dissatisfaction with _____?

What is the cause of the problem you are experiencing?

What does it currently take to manage _____?

Is there anything about your current situation you don't like?

Where do you see a need for improvement?

If you could invent a product or service to solve your problems, what would it do?

Of course, the point is not to ask endless questions or gather infinite information. Each question should clarify the prospect's needs and problems so that informed proposals, accurate recommendations, and compelling presentations can be made.

Implementing *The DNASelling Method*

Training graduates frequently ask, "How am I going to remember to ask all of these questions?" The answer is, of course, "You're not." The sample questions are simply *lists* of potential questions to choose from.

Even the best and brightest sales professionals find it hard to ask effective questions unless they are planned in advance. Excellent questions don't just flow off the top of a salesperson's head while he or she is engaging with prospects. To implement *The DNASelling Method*, sellers need to prepare their questions ahead of time. By selecting a few questions from each category, writing them down, and memorizing them, sellers create a framework to implement *The DNASelling Method*. After memorizing a few questions from each category, sellers can adapt the questions to individual situations. As our training graduates have proven over and over again, with a little bit of time and effort, asking *DNASelling* questions becomes second nature.

Pre-presentation Site Visits

One way to identify the specific needs of buyers is to conduct pre-presentation site visits. In business-to-business presentations, site visits can have enormously positive effects. By visiting the location or facility of a buyer, *prior to presenting* (sometimes even taking official plant or company tours), presenters can meet account players and see first hand the needs and problems buyers are experiencing. The site visit shows a genuine interest in the buyers' business and demonstrates that you care about their needs and problems. You want to help them—not just make a sale.

I learned the power of pre-presentation site visits as a sales executive for a library automation software company. We provided software solutions for educators and school districts. Our presentations involved local and district level technical coordinators, librarians, and principals.

As an executive, I would periodically attend the presentations of our various sales representatives. While attending a presentation in Seattle, Washington, I noticed a sense of coldness on the part of the audience toward our salesperson. Although she was warm and friendly, the audience seemed distant and non-responsive. After the presentation, I commended her for an excellent presentation and discussed with her the almost bizarre response from the audience. In the course of our post-presentation discussion, she made an off hand statement that literally stopped me in my tracks. She said, "That happens to me a lot in Seattle. The local sales rep [competitor] in Seattle always visits the sites before I show up and sours them against me."

I returned to corporate headquarters and began conducting phone and face-to-face interviews with our salespeople. I was stunned to find out that this was a common problem experienced by our sales personnel. I pulled in the sales managers for a "war room" discussion to determine how best to combat this problem. We decided to fight fire with fire. We made pre-presentation site visits a mandatory part of the presentation process. The results were staggering. Sales increased exponentially, and competitors were at a complete loss as to why they were suddenly losing so many sales. Our pre-presentation site visits made all the difference.

We even went a step further and had our salespeople volunteer to help out in the libraries to see first hand the problems and "bottlenecks" educators were experiencing. Based on the visits, our salespeople would incorporate exact situations, names of children and educators they interacted with—even pictures of librarians and teachers taken with digital cameras during the site visit—into the presentation. The bottom line was that the audience could relate to the presenter because he or she demonstrated an interest and understanding of their experience. The presenter had been on the front lines dealing with the problems the buyers were experiencing.

The Point? Site visits provide presenters with an opportunity to build relationships, learn account specific information, and diagnose the exact needs and problems of buyers—prior to presenting.

Pre-presentation site visits offer the following benefits:

1. Meeting and relating to members of an audience prior to the presentation. There won't be any ice to break; traditional introductory resistance will be eliminated, and the presenter will no longer be presenting to strangers.
2. Building relationships and rapport with buyers. Buyers will know the presenter cared enough to take the time to conduct an on-site analysis of their exact needs and problems.
3. Building product sponsors and account champions.
4. Identifying potential "stump the chump" presentation participants.
5. Gathering critical information to personalize the presentation to the precise needs of buyers. By assembling site-specific knowledge, presenters are able to use exact examples and scenarios that relate to the specific circumstances of the participants.
6. Giving the presenter a competitive edge. If competitors do not conduct pre-presentation site visits, they will not have the relationships or necessary information to conduct a presentation that is tailored to the exact situations of the buyer.

Note: The primary benefit of conducting site visits is gaining first hand information that can be used to create customized presentation content.

Conducting Pre-presentation Site Visits

The process of conducting a pre-presentation site visit is extremely important. When we first implemented our site visit policy at the library automation company, we had overzealous sellers who would attempt to "Seek first to be understood, then to understand." They had it backwards. Every time they saw a problem or dilemma, they would jump in and start rattling off how our product could solve the problem. We taught them to avoid this mistake by being cerebral. Instead of jumping in and conducting a premature solution presentation, we trained them to ask questions and take notes.

> **Caution!** The site-visit is not a time to sell or present. This is critical to understand. It is a time to question, listen, observe, and take notes—nothing more.

The essence of sales maturity is a professional's capacity to delay responses, question, and listen. Cerebral selling requires self-control and discipline. The majority of a site visit should be spent asking questions and listening, not giving a laundry list of features or capabilities.

Defeating Competitors with First Hand Information

I was involved in a large sale in Jackson, Mississippi. Due to the size of the sale, multiple vendors were invited to deliver a presentation to a committee of over forty people. It was one of the largest presentations in which I had ever been involved. Prior to the presentation, we conducted site visits to each of the locations involved in the sale. We toured their facilities and asked need-problem questions. We volunteered to help out on the "front lines" to appreciate some of the problems clients experienced. In short, we equipped ourselves with first hand information, which we then used to customize our presentation to the exact needs of the committee members. We exercised the power of CIA (Counter Intelligence & Account-information). It was a beautiful strategy, but there was one problem. Minutes before the presentation was to be delivered, our projector broke! We had no way of providing the participants with a live demonstration of how our software could solve their problems.

Because of the size of the committee, all of the selected vendors were provided one-hour presentation time slots to show their products. There was no second chance. We were forced to deliver a presentation without showing the software. We were devastated. However, we knew we had only one shot and needed to make the most of the opportunity. We decided rather than to show the software, to talk about the problems we had seen on our site visits—in great detail. We dropped the names of the people we visited. We discussed the first hand experiences we had volunteering at their facilities. We talked about how our product would solve their problems, and we discussed the unique capabilities of our software solutions.

It was a landslide victory.

Because of the information we gained in pre-presentation site visits, we were able to verbally demonstrate what our competitors could not. When our competitors heard what had happened, they were shocked. They had spent over a year and a half wining and dining the I.T. director without once visiting the people who were going to be the actual users of the software. They could not believe we were overwhelmingly selected without "showing" our product. They were so bitter about the experience (and because of the size of the sale) that they threatened the buyer with a lawsuit.

We won that sale because of the power we developed in the investigation stage of the sales cycle. We won because of the individualized information we gained in our pre-presentation site visits. Incidentally, we also instilled enormous fear in our competitors.

Pre-presentation Questionnaires

When Meriwether Lewis and co-commander William Clark accepted President Thomas Jefferson's commission to explore the fabled Northwest Passage—a rumored all water route to the Pacific Ocean—they knew they were in for a difficult journey. Prior to leading their Corps of Discovery through the harrowing conditions, they conducted meticulous pre-expedition surveys of the geography, botany, and Indian cultures of the unexplored territory. They studied maps, interviewed frontiersmen, and read books by French, Spanish, and British trappers.

One method of discovery they used was a comprehensive questionnaire that was sent to people who might have useful knowledge of the Missouri River. The survey was so far-reaching that future president William Henry Harrison, then governor of the Territory of Indiana, received it and responded. The questionnaires proved invaluable to the famed excursion by providing crucial information about the terrain and native tribes the explorers encountered.

Like the surveys conducted by the Lewis and Clark expedition, successful presenters do everything within their power to obtain account information prior to presenting.

One way to acquire information is to distribute pre-presentation questionnaires. Pre-presentation questionnaires "survey" decision makers to ensure that accounts are qualified as well as confirm the needs, pains, and problems of buyers. Pre-presentation questionnaires reveal "red flags" and buyer signals that can be used to create strategic outlines and content. (See figure 4.1).

Pre-presentation questionnaires should be faxed or emailed to prospective clients prior to the presentation. They should be brief (no longer than two pages) and relevant to the needs of the buyer. Using pre-presentation questionnaires has the added benefit of getting buyers to invest TIME (Time, Investment, Money & Effort) into the sale.[3]

In Summary

Winning presenters deliver presentations that are relevant to the interests of their clients. They ask questions, conduct site visits, and do what it takes to find ways to personalize presentations to the needs of the audience.

Winning presenters first receive a presentation before delivering a presentation. They know that without understanding client needs and problems, they cannot offer credible solutions or make reliable recommendations. By uncovering critical needs and problems, presenters form professional, consultative relationships with buyers and establish a premise for action *before the presentation is even delivered.*

> **The Point?** Know what your prospect is buying before you begin selling.

3. See Chapter 4 in *Sales-Side Negotiation* to learn how to exercise the power of TIME.

Sample Questionnaire

What [document control] system do you have in place right now?

What problems are you currently experiencing with your existing [document control] system?

Approximately how many [documents] are you controlling?

How many [corporate binders] do you currently maintain at your facility?

On average, how long does it take to approve [a document]?

What areas in your current [document control] system would you like to improve?

How do you currently manage your [master list]?

Do you have suppliers or customers who would like to access your [documents] through a secure Web interface?

What workflow processes would you like your [document control] program to manage?

How many employees do you anticipate accessing the [document control] system?

What would be the ideal [document control] solution from a functionality standpoint?

How many individuals will be attending the presentation? (Please list names and titles)

What timeframe are you looking at to implement a new [document control] system?

Has funding for this project been approved?

What suggestions do you have for me to make the presentation a success?

Figure 4.1

Note: The sample questionnaire was created by *Patrick Henry & Associates, Inc.* for a business that develops document control solutions for manufacturers.

CHAPTER 5

Presentation Logistics

Details are the difference between champions and near champions.

—Coach John Wooden

With the collapse of the Roman Empire in 476 A.D., The Angles (from southern Denmark) and the Saxons (from northwest Germany) invaded, conquered, and colonized most of modern day England. Combined, they become known as Anglo Saxons—a fierce, warlike, and independent race of people.

While in Rome, a young church deacon named Gregory saw a group of young Anglo Saxon slaves being paraded by a merchant in a local market place. Fascinated at the physical beauty of the blonde, fair skinned, blue-eyed children, he inquired about their origin and nationality. The merchant said that they were "Angles" and that they came from the heathen island of Britain. Gregory apparently replied, "Indeed, they look like angels and ought not be pagans."

After being elected Pope, Gregory organized a body of forty monks and missionaries, placed them under the leadership of a Roman priest named Augustine, and in 597 A.D., sent them to the British Isles to convert the Angles and Saxons to Christianity. Augustine sent word to Ethelbert, the Saxon king of Kent, of his pending arrival. What occurred next is one of history's most extraordinary meetings.

Because the Anglo Saxons did not speak Latin, Augustine knew the king would not be impressed without a royal display of regal extravaganza. Leaving nothing to chance, Augustine orchestrated the entire demonstration. On the scheduled day of appearance, King Ethelbert awaited their arrival just off the coasts of Kent. As Augustine and his forty monks made their way from the ocean's shore, they walked slowly toward the king, chanting a solemn litany and carrying a large silver cross in front of them. Next to the silver cross was a huge mural of Christ painted and gilded on a large, upright frame.

King Ethelbert was overwhelmed by Augustine's spectacular display of devotion and piety. He summoned an interpreter and listened to Augustine's oration. In response, King Ethelbert offered a proclamation of his own.

> Because your words are new… I cannot give my assent to them, and leave the customs which I have so long observed, with the whole Anglo Saxon race. But because you have come hither as strangers from a long distance, and as I seem to myself to have seen clearly, that what you yourselves believed to be true and good, you wish to impart to us, we do not wish to molest you; nay, rather we are anxious to receive you hospitably, and to give you all that is needed for your support, nor do we hinder you from joining all whom you can to the faith of your religion.

Augustine was overjoyed by Ethelbert's response and became a devoted friend of the king. Ethelbert was eventually baptized and assisted Augustine in spreading Christianity in England. Later, Augustine was made the Bishop of England and established his headquarters in south England, becoming the first Archbishop of Canterbury.

Planning the Practical Details of a Presentation

Like St. Augustine, experienced presenters know that audio and visual effects can have a major impact on the overall success of a presentation. St. Augustine's presentation was nothing more than a primeval version of an audio-visual display. His audio (chanting) and visual effects (the silver cross and mural of Christ) were meant to influence the overall thinking and emotions of King Ethelbert.

Seemingly effortless presentations are invariably the result of a great deal of preparation and hard work. Like St. Augustine, winning presenters leave nothing to chance and arrange the logistics of a presentation well in advance of their arrival.

Meticulous organization is necessary to accomplish a successful presentation. Carefully planning practical details allows presenters to concentrate on developing and practicing presentation content and delivery, rather than dealing with unforeseen problems. Identifying the size and shape of a room, available audio and visual equipment, and the proposed date and time of the presentation are all logistics that should be determined well in advance of a presentation.

Days and Times

Presentation training attendees frequently ask, "Does the day of the presentation really make that much of a difference?" My answer is a resounding, "Yes, it does."

Many presenters have no control or influence over the date and time of a presentation. It may be that every presentation a speaker delivers is on someone else's timetable. Even so, there are occasions when presenters have input in regards to the scheduling of a presentation. When a presenter chooses days and times, he or she needs to be aware of the impact certain days and hours have on a presentation.

I am by nature a fairly intense person. I have never had a problem keeping an audience's attention, but I learned the distracting power of a Friday afternoon while delivering a presentation in Santa Cruz, California. The presentation started off well , but at around 3 P.M., I could tell I was losing the concentration of the audience. One of the primary decision makers in particular seemed distracted, so I took a risk and asked him, "Hey, is everything O.K.? You seem a bit distracted." He responded, "I'm sorry. My son is in a volleyball tournament tomorrow, and I'm getting the pre-game parent jitters."

A salesperson who delivers a presentation on a Friday risks losing the audience's attention, especially if the presentation is conducted in the afternoon. The simple reality is that people lose their ability to concentrate on Friday afternoons because their minds wander to non-work related, upcoming weekend activities. They've had a long week of work and are looking forward to a couple of days off.

Conducting a presentation on a Monday is also dangerous (particularly Monday mornings). Since Monday is the beginning of the work week, people are typically focused on organizing the week, scheduling meetings, setting up appointments, dealing with employees, putting out last week's fires, etc. Monday is also the most likely time for attendees to be interrupted by phone calls, emergencies, and pressing business.

Caution! Avoid Monday morning and Friday afternoon presentations.

The time of day is also important. The absolute worst time to make a presentation is after lunch. Think about a presentation you've attended that was scheduled immediately after lunch. How hard did you have to work to keep from dozing? How difficult was it to keep your eyes open? More than likely, you felt sluggish and sleepy. People struggle to concentrate after lunch, not because of boredom or indifference. It's just a natural reaction to sitting still after an afternoon meal. People's bodies are using energy for digesting, which physiologically draws energy away from the brain. Medically, this phenomenon is called the "post prandial slump."

If you absolutely must make a presentation following lunch, be sure to schedule a few breaks into the presentation. Having participants stand up and stretch or passing out bottles of cold water can have a stimulating effect on people's energy levels.

Note: The best time to make a presentation is between 9 and 11 A.M. During those hours, attendee alertness is at its peak, allowing them to absorb large doses of information. It's also early enough that attendees are not tired, hungry, or worn out.

Get There on Time

Better three hours too soon than a minute too late.

—Shakespeare

Working out details to ensure an on time arrival at a presentation seems rudimentary, I know. I mention it for one reason—it's a problem. It happens every day in the sales and presentation arena. Every experienced presenter has a war story about showing up late for a presentation. It is the cardinal sin in the presentation industry and kills presentations and sales.

My rookie year in sales, I set up a presentation to a committee of technicians in Denver, Colorado. I identified their critical needs and created a customized presentation. I made sure the UDM's (ultimate decision makers) would be in attendance. I was prepared. I did everything right except get detailed directions to the location. I arrived in Denver and thought I had time to spare. After driving around endlessly looking for the location, I began to panic. I called my contact person to get exact directions, but he had already departed for the presentation location. I drove frantically trying to find the location. When I finally arrived, it was too late. Some of the decision makers had gone, and the remaining attendees seemed perturbed at my tardiness. Who could blame them? It was entirely my fault. I failed to get exact directions to the presentation location. Needless to say, it was a rough presentation, and I lost the sale.

In order to avoid creating your own presentation war stories, the following tips might prove helpful:

- Ask your host to fax or email detailed directions to the location, including a map.
- Have names and phone numbers of several attendees who might be able to assist you in case of an emergency.
- Carry a cellular phone.
- If possible, conduct a pre-presentation site visit to familiarize yourself with the address and location. At least try to make a dry run the day before.

- Calculate travel and departure times to ensure arrival at the presentation location at least an hour before “tip off” time.

Caution! Do not rely on Internet map directories such as *Mapquest* for directions! Although they can be great tools in general, they often provide outdated or incorrect information.

Using Audio Visual Aids

A picture is worth a thousand words.

—Chinese Proverb

Audio-visual (AV) aids can be vital to the success of a presentation. They can highlight important points, emphasize themes, and illustrate difficult concepts more easily than words. Numerous studies show that presentation participants view presenters who use audio and visual aids as more professional and more credible than presenters who merely speak.

Adding visuals such as graphs, charts, maps, or photos to a presentation can also increase the amount of information participants retain. Presentations that are reinforced with audio and visual aids help audience members understand and remember content better, leading to more favorable decisions.

Note: If you show something, people are far more likely to remember it than if you only say something.

There are a variety of AV aids to choose from. Different audio-visual aids suit different types of presentations and have varying levels of complexity.

The following are popular audio-visual aids:

- Computer and video projectors

- Overhead projectors
- Slide projectors
- Whiteboards
- Flipcharts
- Computer graphics
- Posters, banners, and handouts

Computer and video projectors are great audio-visual aids for both large and small crowds. With programs such as Corel's Presentation® and Microsoft's PowerPoint® for the PC, and Keynote® for Macintosh, presenters can create screens, three-dimensional images, graphs, charts, video clips, and moving graphics that enhance both the content and delivery of a presentation.

Many presenters choose to use multiple audio-visual aids in the same presentation. For example, I know presenters who use computer projectors coupled with a portable flipchart to go back and forth between a formal PowerPoint presentation and a live flipchart discussion. "Variety is the spice of life," and using an array of multimedia or audio-visual tools can help keep the attention of participants, highlight key points, and emphasize major themes in numerous ways.

Caution! Used inappropriately, audio-visual aids can actually detract from a presentation. Don't over do it. Keep audio-visual aids simple, clear, and easy to understand.

Keep in mind that audio, visual, and multimedia aids should enhance the message, not become the message. If AV aids are too showy or overwhelming, they can replace the speaker as the main attraction rather than act as a support mechanism. When planning audio, visual, or multimedia presentations, follow a few simple guidelines:

- Make sure that the message is not lost in the glitz and glitter of the audio visual aids.
- Be certain that the graphic images are relevant to the message.

- Avoid using dense text and highly detailed tables and graphs.

Note: The remainder of this chapter focuses on presentations delivered to large audiences.

Lighting and Acoustics

If possible, presenters should visit the chosen presentation site in advance of the presentation. When visiting the location, you should identify any awkward obstructions or limitations that might interfere with the presentation. Issues related to lighting, acoustics, seating, electrical power, and Internet accessibility, should all be carefully considered prior to presenting. If a pre-presentation visit is not practical, get a detailed description of the floor plan or facility.

There will be times when the setup of the room will be completely out of the hands of the presenter. In those cases, make do with what you are given. However, normally the presenter will have the final say about lighting, acoustics, and seating arrangements.

Lighting is especially important when using visual aids. When you are using manual visual aids on whiteboards or flip charts, make certain the light surrounding the visual aid is sufficient for every audience member to see. If you are using a computer, video, or overhead projectors, ensure the lighting can be dimmed for purposes of visibility.

Remember that the most important visual aid is the presenter. Be sure the lighting is adequate for audience members to clearly see you. Facial expressions and body language are effective presentation tools but are of no value if the audience can't see them.

I delivered a presentation to a group of entrepreneurs in Hilo, Hawaii. Over one hundred people attended the presentation. The presentation was delivered on the top floor of a large hotel, and the entire circumference of the room was glass. Audience members had a panoramic view of the local beaches, setting sun, and ocean. It was a beautiful setting. The presentation began at 6:00 P.M., so the room was naturally illuminated from the sun shining through the glass windows. When the sun set, however, the lighting system in the room was insufficient. The room literally turned dark, and audience members from the back of the room could not see my face. What should have been one of my most memorable presentation settings turned out to be one of the most disappointing.

Public Address Systems

Presentations to large audiences require the use of public address (PA) systems. When you use a public address system, check the equipment to ensure that it is functioning properly. Prior to the presentation, familiarize yourself with how the system works, and test it in advance for volume and speaker adjustments. Don't just assume it works. Test the entire system at least an hour before presenting.

Presenters should use clip-on microphones whenever they are available instead of hand held or podium microphones. Clip-on microphones provide mobility and allow presenters to use both hands during the presentation. Podium microphones, on the other hand, restrict a speaker's movement and limit body language and hand gestures.

Be sure to carry spare batteries for all PA accessory parts. While delivering a presentation to over a thousand people in West Palm Beach, Florida, I was reminded that a $2.00 microphone battery can make a $2,000 PA system inoperable.

The Psychology of Seating

One of the most important aspects of presenting is the seating arrangement of audience members. The seating arrangement not only affects the comfort of the audience, but also the relationship between the presenter and the audience.

There is an entire psychology behind seating arrangements. The influence seating can have on participants' perceptions of both the presenter as well as the presentation should not be taken lightly. I have seen seasoned presenters become very heated with hotels and convention centers over the issue of seating arrangements because they know that seating arrangements affect the presentation.

The first and most important seating "rule of thumb" is to ensure that audience members can see the presenter. While I realize this might sound a bit sophomoric, it's not. I have been appalled at the lack of common sense presenters have displayed when setting up the seating arrangement of a room. Sometimes common sense is not common practice.

Chairs and tables should be arranged to ensure optimum visibility of both the speaker and the visual aids. Presentation participants should never have to visually strain or physically adjust in their seats to see the presenter or the visuals.

In large rooms, the most visual-friendly setup is the theatre style, or its slight variation, the chevron style. Traditional theatre styles typically provide three columns of chairs (and tables for the chevron style), with two rows separating the three columns. The two side columns are slanted or angled inward for a better view of the presenter and/or the screen.

Theatre styles are great for training sessions, workshops, seminars, and large sales presentations. The theatre set up is designed for a mobile presenter who likes to move around the room and "work the crowd." It provides the presenter with the greatest opportunity to interact with the audience, make eye contact with participants, and gently touch participants on shoulders and arms while walking down isles.

Use common sense when you make seating arrangements for presentations to small audiences or when presenting around conference tables. My personal preference for a small audience is the semicircle. The semicircle layout provides optimum visibility and contact with the presenter. The only disadvantage of the semicircle is that it takes up a lot of space.

Traditional Theatre Style Seating

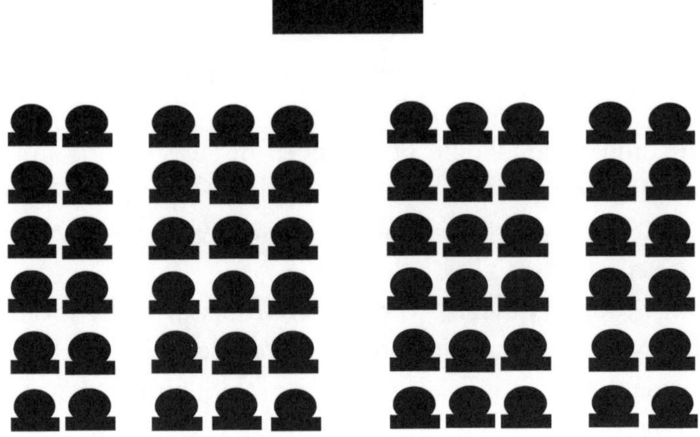

Figure 5.1

Chevron Style Seating

Figure 5.2

Semicircle Seating Layout

Figure 5.3

> **Note:** Seating arrangement rules are not set in stone and neither are the seats. Do not hesitate to move things around to fit the needs and objectives of the presentation.

Audience Perceptions of Seating Arrangements

Empty rooms are horrible settings for presentations. Large numbers of empty chairs communicate to attendees that the presenter was expecting more people to show up. It's like dining at a restaurant that is empty. You begin to question if there is a reason nobody is there.

If there are 100 chairs in a room and only 50 people, attendees will perceive that the presenter was expecting more people. That's bad news for a presenter. If attendees look around and notice a sea of empty chairs, they might begin to wonder if they made a mistake in showing up. On the contrary, if there are 40 chairs, and more chairs are set up as attendees arrive, audience members will perceive a full house and a larger than expected turnout. This generates what is called "Herd Theory," which is the idea that, "Because everyone else is moving in a certain direction, so should I." Herd theory lowers people's perceptions of risk because they are no longer doing something alone.

> **Note:** Attendees perceive audience size not by the number of people in the room, but by the number of empty chairs in the room. The perceived size of an audience is affected by the amount of available space, not the amount of people.

Another problem with empty chairs is that people are scattered throughout the room rather than seated together. When people are scattered throughout a room, it creates what is called the "coliseum effect," making it harder to generate feedback and, more importantly, audience energy.

In order to avoid the coliseum effect, and as a general guideline for seating participants, seat attendees in close proximity to one another. When audience members are sitting close together, they begin to feel and respond like a unified group rather than as isolated individuals.

There are a couple of rules to follow when seating large (more than 25 people) audiences. Rule number one: set up fewer chairs than the number of expected people. If you are expecting 100 people, set up 75 chairs and have 25 chairs stacked in the back of the room as a backup. Rule number two: Tape off the back rows to ensure attendees fill the room from front to back. Simply take masking tape and run a piece of tape from one row to the next, blocking entrance. After people fill up a row (moving from front to back), pull off the tape and fill the next row.

In Summary

Simple, logistical oversights can destroy a presentation. Be sure to address the practical details of a presentation early enough in the process so that adequate time can be spent on content development and delivery rehearsals. Confirm and double check dates and times, room size, audio-visual capabilities, and the exact location of the presentation site.

part two

II

Presentation Content

6. Creating Winning Sales Presentations
7. Developing Powerful Content
8. Strategic Introductions
9. Compelling Messages
10. Memorable Conclusions

CHAPTER 6

Creating Winning Sales Presentations

Luck is the residue of design.

—Vince Lombardi

In 431 B.C., the Greek city-state of Sparta declared war on Athens. The Spartan military state was eager to use its military might to crush the new democratic upstart and its bold leader, Pericles. Pericles was the greatest statesman of ancient Greece and the living symbol of Athenian glory. He introduced new forms of architecture, education, and government. He fostered the full development of Athenian democracy and was responsible for the "Golden Age of Greece." As the general of the Athenian army, Pericles braced Athens for the Peloponnesian War.

Spartan warriors struck first and inflicted a decisive blow against the Athenians.

At the funeral for the dead, after the first battle of the war, Pericles used his eloquence to inspire his Athenian countrymen to fight on.

> Such is the city [Athens] for whose sake these men nobly fought and died. . . in the face of death they resolved to rely upon themselves alone. And when the moment came, they were minded to resist and suffer rather than to fly and save their lives. They ran away from the word of dishonor, but on the battlefield their feet stood fast... this is the solid prize with which, as with a garland, Athens crowns her sons, living and dead, after a struggle like theirs. For where the rewards of virtue are greatest, there the noblest citizens are enlisted in the service of their state.

Pericles' funeral oration both inspired the people of Athens to continue fighting and communicated the necessity of making sacrifices—including the ultimate sacrifice of one's life.

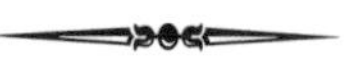

Ancient Greece: A Study of the Art of Persuasion

Ancient Greeks are celebrated for their oratory skill and rhetoric. The political, social, and cultural speeches in ancient Greece are still studied as masterpieces of public speaking, debate, and persuasion.

The Greeks enveloped the art of persuasion in three categories:

1. Ethos (Character and Credibility)
2. Pathos (Emotion and Delivery)
3. Logos (Logic and Content)

Winning sales presentations embody the three pillars of Greek persuasion—ethos, pathos, and logos. When presenters establish character and credibility, use rationale and logic to support their message, and touch the human, emotional side of an audience, they influence the moral, mental, and emotional aspects of a purchasing decision.

Stephen R. Covey states, "The Greeks had a magnificent philosophy which is embodied in three sequentially arranged words: *ethos, pathos,* and *logos*. I suggest these three words contain the essence… of making effective presentations."[1]

Ethos: Character and Credibility

Ethos is the ethical element of a presentation, centering on the character and credibility of a presenter. The greater the credibility of the presenter, the more value participants attach to the information being presented. Without character and credibility, participants will not trust the claims of the presenter or the value of the proposed products or solutions.

1. Stephen R. Covey, *The 7 Habits of Highly Effective People* (New York: Simon and Schuster, 1989) 255.

The first thing a buyer does when listening to a sales presentation is size up the presenter. Is the presenter honest? Does the presenter have integrity? Can I trust this person? Is this person competent? These are all questions audience participants ask themselves during the initial few minutes of a sales presentation. The answers they form can be the difference between winning and losing a sale.

With character and credibility firmly established, buyers advance from evaluating the presenter to evaluating the product or service.

Pathos: Emotion and Delivery

The most important factor of a successful presentation is pathos—the emotion and delivery skills of the presenter. Pathos represents the right brained, imaginative, creative side of a presentation and demonstrates the passion and enthusiasm of the presenter.

Pathos centers on the emotional appeal of a presentation and focuses on a presenter's ability to reach the "hearts" of an audience. Pathos has to do with feelings and represents the emotional communication between presenters and buyers. Because people make purchasing decisions based on both mental and emotional factors, it's important to reach buyers intellectually and emotionally.

I consulted for a company with a team of extremely talented presenters. When I reviewed audiotapes of their top performers, I was amazed at their level of skill and expertise. However, when I listened to audiotapes of their less successful presenters, a glaring difference emerged. The top performers, without exception, touched the emotional side of their audiences. They conveyed case studies, scenarios, and examples with passion and conviction. They injected personal stories that tugged on the sympathies and emotions of buyers. They delivered *balanced* presentations that reached both the intellectual and emotional facets of their audiences. The less successful presenters, on the other hand, were *unbalanced* and focused almost exclusively on the facts, features, and functionality of their offers. They were professional, informative, and delivered content rich presentations, but they failed to reach the hearts and emotions of their audience.

Lacking stimulating delivery skills, presentations are boring, ineffective, and leave participants without a mental or emotional attachment to the presenter or the proposed product or service. This is why winning presenters use delivery skills that influence both the emotional and intellectual side of the decision-making process.

Logos: Logic and Content

Logos deals with the logic and content of a presentation. It is the rational communication that takes place between buyers and sellers. Logical appeals are based on evidence and speak to an audience's intelligence. Logos is the reason and rationale a presenter provides in supporting his or her proposal—the evidence and "left brain" appeal of a presentation. Mr. Spock from *Star Trek,* or Sherlock Holmes, are considered ultimate practitioners of the logical appeal.

Logos deals not only with the logical flow of presented information, but also with the logic of the information itself. The logos part of the presentation answers the "why" and "how" questions about a product or service. Testimonials, product capabilities, unique benefits, and competitive advantages answer these questions and establish the logical foundation of a presentation.

Delivering Balanced Presentations

Effective presentations are balanced. They project integrity, offer mentally engaging material, and touch the emotions of presentation participants. Balanced presentations incorporate the Greek principles of persuasion. They create introductions that establish credibility (ethos), implement delivery skills that build audience feeling and rapport (pathos), and use presentation content that is organized, logical, and easy to understand (logos).

The Point? People buy emotionally and justify their decisions logically. The most effective way to impact an audience, therefore, is to offer a combination of both logical and emotional appeals.

Three Objectives of a Sales Presentation

Memorable sales presentations don't happen by accident. They are strategically planned, organized, and structured to make a favorable impression, deliver easily remembered benefits, and ultimately sell a product or service.

Sales presentations have three ultimate objectives:

1. Impression
2. Retention
3. Selection

Impression is what audience participants think and feel about you and your product or service. *Retention* is what they remember about you and your product or service while *selection* is whether or not they choose your product or service.

In order to make a powerful sales presentation, strategies and content must be designed prior to delivery. An important part of any presentation strategy is to establish a presentation theme or thesis. How many talks, speeches, or presentations have you attended where you didn't know what the point was before, during, or after the presentation? Listening to a presentation without a theme or thesis can be extremely frustrating.

All great presentations have a theme or message. Sales presentations are no exception and need to be organized so that buyers can easily identify the point of the presentation. The point might be an exclusive feature, unique capability, or competitive advantage. Unfortunately, far too many presenters are unprepared with no strategy or identifiable theme. They just "show up and throw up" on participants hoping that kind of, sort of, maybe, on a good day, with a down hill wind, buyers will choose their product or service.

Winning presenters don't leave anything to chance. They strategically organize presentations with easily remembered benefits that lead to favorable impressions, content retention, and product or service selection.

Making a Favorable Impression

Making a favorable impression and captivating the minds and hearts of presentation participants is one of the primary purposes for delivering a sales presentation. Because this is so important, when you organize presentation content, remember that every part of the presentation needs to help achieve this objective.

Of course, presentation delivery is a vital part of creating a favorable impression. All the same, the content and structure of the presentation are equally important. Organized thoughts and expressions leave positive feelings and affirmative impressions with audience participants. Remember that the opposite is also true. Unorganized thoughts and pointless expressions create negative impressions and doubt in the minds of buyers.

When presentations are communicated with effective delivery skills, are strategically structured to emphasize competitive advantages, and have a clear and retainable theme, participants are left with favorable impressions of both the presenter and the proposed product or service.

> **Caution!** Confused prospects don't buy. Unorganized, confusing, or illogical presentations leave buyers without clear and compelling reasons to purchase proposed products or services.

Content Retention

If you can't explain it simply, you don't understand it well enough.

—Albert Einstein

Fostering content retention is no easy task. Many studies have demonstrated that within seven days of a presentation most disseminated information is forgotten. Increasing content retention is possible, though, by following a few, simple guidelines:

1. Emphasize a limited number of presentation points or benefits.
2. Organize the highlighted points or benefits into a structured arrangement.
3. Repeat highlighted points of emphasis.

Most presentations overwhelm participants with too much information, too many facts, graphs, features, and capabilities. Winning presenters understand that sometimes *less is more.* Emphasizing a limited number of points or benefits—typically between three and five—is more effective than overloading buyers with too much information.

The Point? Organize presentation content and structure the body of a presentation in a way that emphasizes easily remembered points and benefits.

The Laws of Memorable Impact

In the early 1900's, scientists began studying nuclear particles. During the research, they discovered that the radioactivity in most nuclear substances dissipates naturally over time. They measured this phenomenon in units of half-life—the time required for nuclear material to lose half its radioactive energy. Some nuclear substances have a half-life of less than one millionth of a second, while others lose half their radiation in millions of years.

The same phenomenon happens with human memory. Although we would like to think that buyers remember everything we present, much of the information naturally dissipates over time. The half-life of a sales presentation is measured in hours and days, not weeks and months.

To increase content retention, presenters need to be aware of limitations associated with intellectual erosion and follow fundamental rules of memory retention.

There are three laws associated with memory retention:

1. Law of Primacy: People remember what they hear first.
2. Law of Frequency: People remember what they hear most.
3. Law of Recency: People remember what they hear last.

To increase content retention, you should introduce points and themes in the introduction of the presentation (law of primacy), emphasize them in the body of the presentation (law of frequency), and highlight them again at the conclusion of the presentation (law of recency).

How many times do you have to hear a song before you remember the lyrics? The general rule is between five and eight times. Remembering the lyrics to a song is not much different than remembering the key points of a presentation. The key is repetition. Skilled presenters repeat easily remembered product or service benefits throughout their presentations.

Winning presenters understand that what counts is not what is said, but what is remembered. In order to increase retention, presenters need to follow the laws of memory retention by reinforcing critical points of discussion and repeating them multiple times.

Note: Recapping information is an important way of reinforcing the main points of a presentation. When structuring presentations, build repetition into the framework.

While teaching this principle, I am frequently asked, "How do you repeat easily remembered benefits without sounding annoyingly repetitive?" The key is to be creative, using a variety of media, and appropriately spacing the repetition. For example, while presenting our advanced sales and presentation training, I purposely repeat my primary theme (that sales professionals lacking presentation skills consistently lose otherwise winnable sales) in my introduction, again in the body of my presentation, and a third time in my conclusion. By spacing my theme throughout the presentation, I am able to emphasize my primary point without beating it to death.

Simply repeating the same information, however, is normally not adequate. Presenters need to be creative and use different phrasing to keep ideas sounding fresh and engaging.

Presenters should use several mediums of communication to reach as many senses as possible. Obviously, in a presentation, voice (audio) is most important. Verbally highlighting a point of emphasis using vocal inflection aids retention, but this is usually not enough. Adding visual aids such as images, graphs, charts, and testimonials on a large screen will help reinforce the highlighted point. Handouts are also useful to reinforce and repeat the major points of emphasis.

> **The Point?** Using a variety of presentation tools such as voice inflection, images, charts, graphs, testimonials, and handouts can help participants remember key points, unique benefits, and competitive differential advantages.

The Rule of Three

People remember things better when they are presented in groups of three. For reasons not fully understood, human memory retains things more clearly when they are associated with related words, topics, or subjects in sets of three. Think of witty quotes or sayings that you can remember off the top of your head. How about, "Healthy, wealthy, and wise," or "Morning, noon, and night." "The good, the bad, and the ugly." Bible readers will recognize, "Gold, frankincense, and myrrh."

Whatever the explanation, people are more apt to remember ideas and concepts when they are presented in sets of three. This mnemonic phenomenon is referred to as "The rule of three." The rule of three is a retention technique that groups three words, ideas, or concepts into one sentence or phrase. Popular illustrations of this phenomenon include:

> *I came. I saw. I conquered.*
>
> —Julius Caesar

> *Government of the people, by the people, for the people.*
>
> —Abraham Lincoln

> *The Holy Roman Empire was neither holy, nor Roman, nor an empire.*
>
> —Voltaire

When creating content, organize major points of discussion, themes, or benefits into groups of three. For example, a presenter might state in both the introduction and conclusion of a presentation, "The benefits of doing business with ABC Company can be summed up in three sentences: Better product. Better support. Better price." You might also use: "Better technology. Better service. Better results."

I consulted with a company that provides Internet marketing strategies that are nothing short of brilliant. After reviewing their PowerPoint sales presentation, I recommended that they shorten their presentation and narrow their laundry list of features and capabilities into three simple benefits: Customized Web site design, Internet-specific marketing training, and ongoing support. It worked fabulously. Rather than leaving the presentation confused or overwhelmed, prospects understood and remembered the exact capabilities and benefits the company offered.

When teaching this principle, I often start the training by casually mentioning what I ate for breakfast. I will tell the training participants that I ate an apple, an orange, and a banana for breakfast. At the end of the day, and to make the point, I will ask the audience, "How many of you remember what I had for breakfast this morning?" Inevitably, 90 percent of the audience will say, "An apple, an orange, and a banana."

The Point? Make three points that stick, rather than ten points that leave no lasting impression. Keep major points of emphasis in groups of three.

In Summary

Adult audiences have a limited attention span of about one hour. During that hour they will absorb about a third of what is said and will remember a maximum of five points.

When you are creating presentation content, limit the number of major points to keep the message clear and memorable. Emphasize major points or benefits at the beginning of the presentation, in the middle, and again at the end. Follow the laws of memorable impact and organize key concepts into groups of three for maximum retention.

CHAPTER 7

Developing Powerful Content

Everything should be made as simple as possible, but not simpler.

—Albert Einstein

Johann Sebastian Bach, Wolfgang Amadeus Mozart, and Ludwig van Beethoven are three of the most accomplished composers in history. Each man made an indelible mark on classical music. They were German and lived in roughly the same era, but each of them orchestrated sounds and harmonies that were completely distinct and unique to his own personality. Bach, for example, was only five feet tall. Nevertheless, he had a giant intellect, passionate personality (he had twenty children), and an overpowering presence that was reflected in his music. A devoted Lutheran, he integrated his deep religious convictions into his melodies. He is perhaps best known for his composition, *Toccata and Fugue in D Minor for Organ*.

Mozart, unlike Bach, was foul-mouthed and socially distasteful. He had an odd fondness for shocking people with his love of swearing and uncouth behavior. He was, by traditional standards, unconventional, brilliant, and eccentric, as was his music. He created a distinct sound known for its mastery of form and richness of harmony. He composed symphonies, operas, concertos, sonatas, and choral and chamber pieces, and is credited with over six hundred works in his brief life (he died at the age of thirty-five). Mozart's most famous works include his *Serenade in G Major, Symphony No. 40 in G Minor, and Concerto No. 21 in C Major for Piano and Orchestra.*

Although Bach and Mozart created profound musical masterpieces, none can compare to Beethoven's *Symphony No. 5 in C Minor.* The combination of power and gentleness in the first movement of *Symphony No. 5* represents the most famous four notes in all of classical music—dot, dot, dot, dash. (Coincidentally, the rhythm of these four notes spells out V in Morse code and came to symbolize VICTORY during World War II). Beethoven's opening rhythm in *Symphony No. 5* is the most recognized classical phrase ever created. Its distinct harmony and unique sound establishes a presence that is both captivating and engaging.

Developing Powerful Presentations

Like the great composers of the past, high earning sales professionals create presentations that are powerful, memorable, and engaging. Similar to a musician composing a melody, successful sellers rehearse and refine their presentation until, like Beethoven, they develop their own "masterpiece."

For most salespeople, presenting is the most exciting part of the selling process. It is also the most challenging. Delivering high impact presentations is no easy task. The presenting stage, more than any other stage of the sales cycle, requires the greatest skill. This stage most influences the success or failure of a sale.

Successful presentations are the result of training, practice, and adequate rehearsal. As any seasoned sales professional will attest to, creating and delivering an effective presentation is anything but simple. Presenters need a solid understanding of the elements of a successful presentation, a grasp of the latest presentation technologies, and a plan for creating powerful presentation content.

To help systematize the presentation stage of the selling process, *Patrick Henry & Associates* provides a five-step procedure for developing effective outlines and delivering successful presentations. Using this five-step process, presenters:

1. Identify buyer needs and problems (using *The DNASelling Method*)
2. Create a *Presentation Pedigree* (matching buyer needs to product solutions)
3. Develop a presentation outline

4. Rehearse and refine presentation content
5. Deliver the presentation

Using *The DNASelling Method*, site visits, questionnaires, and previous sales conversations, cerebral sellers first identify the prospect's primary buying motives. They then match the needs and problems of decision makers to product solutions, using the *Presentation Pedigree* to compile the information into a presentation outline. After rehearsing and refining the content, they deliver the presentation.

The Winning Sales Presentation Development Model

Figure 7.1

Step 1: Identify Buyer Needs and Problems

As I addressed in Chapter 4, successful sales presentations are based on the specific needs, concerns, and interests of buyers. Conducting a thorough needs-analysis and identifying the issues that are important to buyers is the cornerstone of any effective sales presentation.

Winning presenters use *The DNASelling Method*, conduct site visits, and utilize other information gathering activities to obtain information they will include in a presentation.

Step 2: Create a Presentation Pedigree

Once needs, problems, and primary buying motives have been identified, sellers need to determine the solutions that address the needs and solve the problems. To assist sellers in this process, *Patrick Henry & Associates* provides the *Presentation Pedigree*. The *Presentation Pedigree* helps sellers match core competencies and unique solutions to the specific needs and motives of buyers. Filling in the *Presentation Pedigree*, sellers chart the core components of a successful presentation. They identify ultimate decision makers, their needs and problems, and the corresponding solutions, features, and benefits that are unique to their product or company.

Electronic Presentation Pedigrees

Patrick Henry & Associates provides an electronic version of the Presentation Pedigree that walks a salesperson through the process of determining the content critical to a winning presentation. Upon completion of a Presentation Pedigree for a given account, the salesperson organizes the content or scenarios into a chronological order that makes sense. The electronic *Presentation Pedigree* is a module within SONAR (see www.sonarsales.com), that combines steps one, two, and three of The Winning Presentation Development Model into a single, seamless process and provides presenters with automated, *sales-ready* messages.

Using the electronic *Presentation Pedigree,* presenters:

1. Identify decision makers.
2. Determine their needs and primary buying motives.
3. Pinpoint response blocks necessary to overcome product weaknesses or tactics used by the competition.
4. Select and arrange corresponding features, capabilities, and solutions.
5. Create and position examples, stories, and scenarios to highlight selected features, benefits, and solutions.
6. Strategically place the examples, stories, and scenarios in the introduction, message, or conclusion of the presentation.

Once pedigree information is entered, sellers can organize the scenarios and response blocks into a coherent outline for rehearsal and delivery purposes.

An important part of the electronic version of the *Presentation Pedigree* is the *unique* column. Once a feature, benefit, or capability is determined to be unique—meaning no other competitor offers the same feature, functionality, or benefit—it should be strategically positioned in the presentation outline and emphasized in the actual presentation. Using pull-down menus, the electronic *Presentation Pedigree* helps sellers identify and emphasize unique selling points and competitive advantages.

Scenario Selling

In his essay *On Memory and Reflection*, Aristotle makes the statement, "It is impossible to even think without a mental picture." Because humans think in terms of language and imagery, the most effective way to communicate is to use stories and scenarios that invoke mental pictures and images—specifically images that involve the use and application of the presented product or service.

Step four of the *Presentation Pedigree* is to develop and position examples, stories, and scenarios to highlight selected features, benefits, and solutions. These scenarios are examples that illustrate the power of a presented product or service. For example, based on a site visit, conversation, or questionnaire, a presenter can use a factual scenario or experience to illustrate a point. By using the situations, experiences, and scenarios of presentation participants (and existing clients), presenters can address the specific needs, pains, and problems that participants face. This strategy is referred to as "Scenario Selling."

As a sales manager, I observed one of our top salespeople use the scenario selling strategy to deliver a presentation to a committee of librarians. "I noticed while volunteering in the Lincoln high school library that [Mary] cannot currently process fines for late returns without closing her existing check-in-check-out program and opening up a separate fine tracking program. Let me illustrate how our product solves that time consuming dilemma. Let's say that [Mary] has a line of ten students checking out books, and when one of the student's library cards is scanned, it shows an overdue book with a late fee that has yet to be collected. Currently, [Mary] has to close her library automation program, open her tracking program, process the fine, close the fine program, open the check-in-check-out program, and resume her check in process—all while the class bell is ringing with students standing in line waiting to have their books checked out. Now, let me demonstrate how our product solves that frustration in one simple step."

Vivid, authentic scenarios and examples influence decision-makers more than abstract information. Real-life scenarios touch both the minds and hearts of participants. This is why winning presenters attach a particular feeling to the scenario that they would like buyers to feel—frustration, irritation, stress, fear, or maybe even relief. Whatever feelings the scenario invokes, the example is meant to support the value of the proposed solution. By creating scenarios that participants can relate to, presenters create a favorable climate for the proposed solution.

Note: People are much more interested in scenarios than they are in plain facts. Graphs, charts, and statistics do not move people. Scenarios, stories, and examples do. Dramatize proposed solutions with customer-centered scenarios.

Scenario selling is powerful for the following reasons:

- Scenario selling leads to greater message impact and retention.
- Scenario selling adds life to a presentation.

Scenario selling is powerful for the following reasons:

- Scenario selling leads to greater message impact and retention.
- Scenario selling adds life to a presentation.
- Scenario selling makes a presenter stand out from competing vendors.
- Scenario selling adds a refreshing change of pace from the traditional "same old, same old" presentation styles.
- Scenario selling reaches both the mental and emotional factors of a buying decision.

Scenarios that involve customers are particularly powerful. By relating scenarios about existing clients who previously experienced pains and problems similar to the attendees, presenters can drive home the value of proposed products and solutions. For instance, instead of simply explaining or demonstrating a product or service capability, a presenter might weave a reference story or experience of another client into the example or demonstration. Reference scenarios are short, concise examples that focus on how other customers have successfully solved a problem with the capabilities being presented.

> **The Point?** Use the presentation pedigree process to create examples, stories, and scenarios to highlight the features and benefits of the proposed product or service.

Step 3: Develop a Presentation Outline

After filling in the *Presentation Pedigree*, incorporate the information into a presentation outline. (For sellers using the electronic version of the *Presentation Pedigree*, an outline is automatically created). An outline is like a blueprint for a building. It provides the framework and basic structure of a presentation. It helps organize thoughts, themes, and topic chronology. If necessary, the outline can be used as a reference tool *during* a presentation. By creating outlines, presentations are organized but not scripted. Organization fosters credibility and because the presentation is not scripted, a desirable level of spontaneity exists throughout.

> **Note:** Sales presentations need to be carefully mapped and choreographed to ensure that every hot button, competitive advantage, and unique benefit is presented in the most powerful way possible.

There are three sections of a winning presentation: the introduction, the message, and the conclusion. The introduction builds credibility and establishes the tone and direction of the presentation. The message supplies the details and supporting evidence. The conclusion summarizes and highlights the primary points of emphasis.

The major points of a presentation outline are organized alphabetically—A, B, C, and D. Subheading or supporting data are then placed under each major point and are labeled with Arabic numerals, 1, 2, 3, etc. Subheadings provide supporting data that builds evidence and verifies claimed product or service assertions. When needed, secondary subheadings are labeled with Roman numerals, such as i), ii), iii), and so on, followed by lower case alphabetical identifiers—a, b, c, etc.

The following structure is recommended.

A. Topic, Feature, Capability, Benefit, or Competitive Advantage
  1. Supporting Evidence
    i) Scenario, Story, Example, Demonstration, Testimonial
    ii) Scenario, Story, Example, Demonstration, Testimonial
      a. Topic Summary

Sales personations cannot be a bunch of haphazard ideas and recommendations. The presentation must be clearly organized to cover major points or benefits in a coherent order.

SONAR Presentation Outline

Presentation Outline for Jefferson High School

Introduction

1. Introduce yourself: Name, Title, Professional Experience & Expertise
2. Refer to the Timeframe
3. Set the Agenda
4. Deliver a Corporate Capabilities Statement
   a. Company Background
   b. Company Experience & Expertise
   c. Intangible Corporate Benefits
5. (Optional) Quickly Review Client Needs, Pains, or Problems

Content

Top 10 Needs	Pain	Solution	Benefit	Alexandria	Maximus	Velocity	Prestige	Scenario	Story	Testimonial	Presentation	Maximus Response Block	Velocity Response Block	Prestige Response Block
1. SIF Capabilities	Limited data sharing and program interaction. Time requirements necessary to import, export and enter data for each application.	SIF Compatibility	Uniform school database system, accurate student information, consistent patron data and time savings.	X		X	X	X	X	X		X	X	
2. Catalog Authority Control	Duplicate records, catalog inconsistency, duplicate purchases, wasted funds, no standardization	Central Authority Control Module	Better search results - accurate, consistent, quality catalog.	X	X		X	X	X	X			X	X
3. 24/7 Technical Support	High support costs, per call charges, being placed on hold and/or the inability to gain immediate access to a competent technical support person is extremely frustrating.	Toll Free, 24/7 Technical Support	Business, weekend and after hours technical support leads to faster problem resolution, better product utilization and higher productivity.	X				X	X	X				

Figure 7.2

Sonar Presentation Outline Cont'd

4. Thin Clients	Schools with high numbers of computers bog down the network. This results in slow cataloging, check-in, check-out processes and client search results.	Network Bandwith Optimization	Faster network processing, lower bandwith utilization.	X	X	X	X					X	X	X
5. Resource Sharing	Inability to fill patron requests. Limited access to books and periodicals throughout district. Unnecessary duplication of items with limited usage/popularity.	Central Union Catalog	Access to resources from libraries throughout the district. Ability to search, view and reserve district resources with any library with access to the Central Union Catalog.	X	X	X	X	X	X	X		X	X	X
6. MARC Record Search Access	Manually cataloging records is extremely time intensive. Additionally, manually entered MARC records are vastly inferior to to records copied from reputable sources.	Drag & Drop MARC Search Capabilities	Quick, cost effective, easy means of aquiring MARC records	X		X	X	X	X			X	X	
7. Online Updates	Without remote update capabilities, district techncians are often forced to travel to each individual school to update local servers and technology resulting in lost time, delayed upgrades and frustrated librarians.	Instant, Online Updates & Upgrades	Easier, faster access to updated program releases. Less downtime, faster upgrades, improved products and happier librarians.		X	X	X					X	X	X
8. Centralized Reporting	Excessive time required to gather and compile district-wide library data	Central Reporting Module	Accurate, up-to-date, district-wide reports created with the click of a mouse. Better purchasing decsions based on book and periodical use. Huge time saver for District Librarian.	X				X	X	X				
9. Remote Access to Catalog	Teachers and students unable to access library catalog from home, public library or classroom	Browser-based Interface	Better visibility, and increased accessibility to library catalog. Increased use of library resources. Job security for librarian.	X	X	X	X	X	X			X	X	X
10. Interface Customization	Elementary search windows not suited for middle and high school students	Customizable GUI	Local adaptability and control. Ability for Librarians to cutomize interfaces for different age and grade groups	X	X			X	X	X				X

Conclusion

1. Summarize Hot Points and Competitive Differential Advantages
2. Compelling Closing Sentence
3. Transition to Close

Figure 7.3

Step 4: Rehearse and Refine Presentation Content

In 776 B.C., the Greeks instituted the first Olympic Games. Held every four years on the plains of Olympus in honor of Zeus, the games continued for more than a millennium and included patriotic and religious rituals as well as athletic contests. The games became such a central part of Greek culture that the Greeks counted their years in Olympiads (periods of four years) and dated events from the first Olympics.

In 394 A.D., however, the Roman emperor Theodosius put a stop to the games. A Christian convert, Theodosius considered the games to be a scandalous glorification of Greek gods and pagan culture. For the next fifteen hundred years, the Olympics were little more than a forgotten memory in Greek mythology.

When French baron Pierre de Coubertin proposed reviving the Olympic ideal in 1892, he single-handedly convinced thirteen nations to participate in the first modern Olympiad in 1896. Three hundred and eleven male athletes (women were excluded in the first modern Olympics) gathered in Athens, Greece, and competed for their nations.

Unbeknownst to the world, however, Coubertin had an ulterior motive for reinstating the Olympic Games. His purpose was not to win gold medals and glory—it was to improve the physical fitness of the French so that his countrymen would be better prepared in the event of war with Germany. In 1889, the French government commissioned Coubertin to report on the physical fitness of the nation's population and suggest methods to promote what it called "physical culture." As Coubertin traveled across Europe and North America studying the physical education programs of various nations, he became alarmed at the substandard level of physical fitness of the French. He determined that sporting events would rejuvenate the athletic vigor, competitiveness, and physical preparedness of his people. Knowing that hostilities with Germany were inevitable, Coubertin used the Olympic

Games as a way to prepare his people for war. His foresight proved prophetic because within twenty years of the first Olympic Games, France was involved in a world war against Germany.

Rehearsing and refining presentation content is a mandatory part of delivering exceptional presentations. Like Coubertin's use of the Olympics to prepare his countrymen for war, presenters use whatever time and tools they have available to prepare effective content and refine delivery skills.

Similar to Olympic athletes, high performance presenters leave nothing to chance. Olympic sprinters and swimmers win races that are won in seconds, not hours. Think of how much time it takes to prepare to run a one hundred meter dash. The race is won in less than ten seconds. How much preparation goes into winning the race? How many hours do athletes spend weight lifting, practicing, stretching, and running?

Karl Malone, the former All Star power forward for the Utah Jazz, publicly criticized his teammates for showing up to summer camp out of shape. He knew that what takes place in the off-season determines what takes place in the regular season. Presenting is much the same. Presenters need to prepare to be successful. Presenters who are less prepared will be less successful, and presenters who are unprepared will be unsuccessful.

When they rehearse and refine presentation content, presenters implement account specific strategies. Going through the mental process of creating, editing, and rehearsing presentation outlines allows presenters to fine tune their message by developing key words and phrases, positioning unique capabilities, and intentionally placing stories, scenarios, and examples for strategic moments in the presentation.

In addition to practice, winning presenters use modern technology to improve their presentation and delivery skills. I attempt to video or audiotape every presentation I deliver. I review my audio recordings in my car while driving, and my video recordings at home. I am constantly amazed that what I sound and look like on tape is so disparate from what I think I sound and look like. Because most of us are our own worst critics, video and audiotapes enable us to identify and correct mistakes prior to delivering future presentations.

While conducting corporate presentation trainings, one technique *Patrick Henry & Associates* uses is having participants record a short presentation on videotape. We will often set up a video camera and have participants recite a short poem or historical speech such as the Gettysburg Address. We then have participants critique their own performance. Consistently, people are surprised at their voice, body language, facial expressions, or hand and arm gestures. In many cases, participants are not aware that they are moving or that they are gesturing with their hands. Other times they are surprised at the tone of their voice or the facial expressions they make. Based on their own critique, and with the help of our presentation consultants, participants are able to correct or alter undesirable delivery behaviors.

> **The Point?** Winning presenters understand there are no second chances when it comes to presenting. You get one shot to advance the sale. Ensure that you make the most of the opportunity by rehearsing and refining presentation content.

Step 5: Deliver the Presentation

Identifying critical account needs and creating winning presentation outlines is a means to an end. The most essential element of a presentation is the delivery skills of the presenter. Delivery skills add life and meaning to the content. This is why winning presenters share common delivery attributes. They show passion and enthusiasm for their product or service. They are positive and optimistic, communicate confidence, utilize effective humor, and use appropriate amounts of voice inflection, eye contact, and body language.

Delivery skills can be the difference between winning and losing a sale. Because of the importance of delivery skills, I have devoted an entire chapter to the subject. (See Chapter 11).

Referencing Outlines

Winston Churchill developed a reputation for always being meticulously prepared with notes and outlines when addressing the British Parliament or delivering a political speech. However, he rarely actually utilized or referenced his notes. He was once asked by a journalist why he had notes during his presentations but seldom looked at them. Churchill replied, "I carry fire insurance, but I don't expect my house to burn down."

Winston Churchill's response illustrates the primary advantage associated with using notes and outlines. Similar to an insurance policy, notes and outlines act as a back up system to a fickle memory or a forgetful mind.

Many presenters are hypersensitive about the issue of having an audience watch them pause and visually scan an outline. This heightened sensitivity is unwarranted. When presenters pause, take a sip of water, and simultaneously scan an outline, there is no negative effect whatsoever. If anything, it shows that the presenter actually took the time to create an outline in the first place. It projects organization and preparation.

Outlines provide two basic benefits. First, they help sellers organize strategic content. Second, they can be referenced during the presentation as a back up to a foggy memory, or to get back on track when a presenter gets flustered or loses his or her train of thought.

I taught this principle to a team of sales professionals and spent a full day training, role-playing, and practicing presentation skills. In the group was a sales "veteran" who felt he was beyond the need of using and referencing a presentation outline. He felt that outlines were for novice sellers inexperienced in the art of persuasion. His arrogance exceeded his intellect. As the day progressed, he refused to fully participate in the training and neglected to create a presentation outline. When it came time for each person to deliver a three-minute presentation to the other participants, he choked.

Note: There is an enormous difference between "canned" and "planned" presentations. Outlines that are referenced and verbally rehearsed are planned. Outlines that are obviously read are canned.

One of the most successful presenters I know physically holds up his outline at the beginning of his presentations and says, "To ensure that I don't forget any major points today, I am going to be referencing this outline. Is everybody OK with that?" Of course, the audience readily agrees. He then periodically pauses to look over his outline. When I asked him why he uses this strategy he told me, "Because it makes me look human and builds audience rapport." Judging from his results, he is exactly right.

I refer to non-outlined presentations as, "mumbling, stumbling, and fumbling." Presenters who neglect to develop outlines end up not only rambling, but also drifting from the point or theme of their presentation. They neglect to match buyer needs to product solutions. They lose their train of thought, and they lose momentum. They go "off road" and end up confusing potential buyers.

Elite presenters (without exception) create outlines prior to presenting. They don't rely on chance or luck to make powerful presentations. They don't count on their ability to come up with effective ideas and themes off "the top of their heads." As every seasoned presenter will attest, it's impossible to be on your mental "A" game every presentation.

When referencing presentation outlines, be sure not to read from them directly. Notes and outlines are presentation reference tools. That's it. They should be used as guidelines to avert presenters from unintentionally excluding major product or service benefits or critical points of discussion.

The Point? Do not present without first preparing an outline. Outlines make presentations more effective, persuasive, and successful. Without an outline, presentations are longer, wordier, and stray from the point of the presentation.

Using Notepads, Index Cards, or 8 ½ x 11 Paper Sheets

When using notepads or index cards for outlines, I recommend first using the *Presentation Pedigree* process to create a full draft of the presentation, including all major points, scenarios, and examples. Once you create the draft, edit and re-edit the draft until you're satisfied with the content, flow, and pace of the presentation. Choose key words and phrases and incorporate them into the outline.

Although many successful presenters use notepads or index cards to create outlines, I prefer to use traditional 8 1/2 x 11 sheets of paper inserted into paper protectors. These sheets limit the amount of paper or cards that you might have to handle or reference during the presentation. They also give you two full pages (front and back) to create a general or comprehensive outline. Using a two-sided, full-page outline gives a presenter enough room to include as much detail as needed. A double sided presentation outline is like a football "game sheet" that coaches carry on the sidelines and reference during games. The game sheet is a condensed version of the game plan, complete with predetermined offensive plays and defensive schemes based on scouting reports. Like "game sheets," presentation outlines address each major point of the presentation game plan.

> **Note:** Remember that outlines used as reference tools need to be easy to read at a glance. Be sure to keep outline content simple and easy to visually reference.

Using PowerPoint as an Outline

Many presenters use PowerPoint and other electronic presentation tools to create outlines. These products can help presenters stay on track by sequencing projected screens to match the presentation outline.

Although these programs are great audio-visual products, they are limited reference tools. The reason? If presenters only use PowerPoint slides as their outline, and they get flustered, lose their train of thought, or forget major points of discussion, their only real option is to click to the next screen. This means that they might verbally miss or skip vital parts of a presentation. Using PowerPoint for PC's or Keynote for Macintosh computers, presenters cannot look at all the slides simultaneously without closing and opening multiple program windows or "sliding" the screens up and down. When sellers use PowerPoint or Keynote as their exclusive outline, they cannot quickly glance at the entire body of the presentation.

If you use PowerPoint or other audio-visual presentation tools, it is wise to use them in conjunction with a written outline.

In Summary

Winning presenters express organized thoughts and concepts that flow from a structured outline. They use the recommended five-step presentation development process to design messages with identifiable points of emphasis and easily remembered benefits. They create logical, strategic outlines that lead to better understanding, increased comprehension, and improved communication—all of which leads to successful presentations and increased sales.

> **The Point?** Don't leave presentation success to chance. Use the power presentation development model to design outlines that address buyer needs, highlight exclusive product capabilities, and emphasize competitive differential advantages.

Chapter 8

Strategic Introductions

The beginning is the most important part of any work, for that is the time at which the character is formed and the desired impression more readily taken.

—Plato

Margaret Thatcher, Prime Minister of Great Britain, briskly walked into the House of Commons. As she entered, a hushed silence filled the room. It was April 3, 1982, and the British parliament was meeting in its first emergency session in more than 25 years. The moment was intense for both Great Britain and the prime minister.

The day before, without advanced warning, the Argentine government had invaded and conquered the Falkland Islands, one of Britain's last, overseas territories. The United Kingdom had exercised sovereignty over the island since its discovery by Captain Cook off the coast of Argentina in 1775.

Prime Minister Thatcher was in a precarious position. Not only did she face a delicate foreign policy dilemma, but her opposition, the Labour Party, was using the unexpected disaster as a political opportunity to at least embarrass her, and at most unseat her. To make matters worse, the Falkland event followed a recent poll that showed her public approval rating at a new low of just 25%. She knew that to withstand the oncoming attacks, she would have to take a bold and unwavering stance on the Falkland crisis. There was no room for error.

As she began her address to the House of Commons, members of the Labour Party immediately began shouting, "Resign, resign!" Undeterred, she delivered one of Britain's most memorable speeches.

> We are here because, for the first time for many years, British sovereign territory has been invaded by a foreign power. After

> several days of rising tension in our relations with Argentina, that country's armed forces attacked the Falkland Islands yesterday and established military control… Argentina has, of course, long disputed British sovereignty over the islands. We have absolutely no doubt about our sovereignty… Nor have we any doubt about the unequivocal wishes of the Falkland Islanders, who are British in stock and tradition, and they wish to remain British in allegiance… They are few in number, but they have the right to live in peace, to choose their own way of life and to determine their own allegiance… It is the wish of the British people and the duty of Her Majesty's Government to do everything that we can to uphold that right. That will be our hope and our endeavor and, I believe, the resolve of every Member of the House.

Facing such overwhelming opposition, a less determined person might have cracked under the pressure. Instead, Margaret Thatcher delivered a thunderous speech that silenced her critics and rallied the British populace behind her cause. There was, she believed, a principle worth fighting for: aggression must not be tolerated. Following her address, she sent out a fleet of 98 ships that carried 8,000 fighting men over 8,000 miles to a stormy corner of the Atlantic to take back the Falkland Islands.

Her firm stance and resolute words had the desired effect. Seventy-four days later, a British commander accepted the surrender of the Argentine troops in the Falkland Islands.

Introductions Matter

Margaret Thatcher's address to the House of Commons is an example of a speaker starting an address with a clear and unmistakable introduction. Her language, content, and delivery conveyed a message of power in the face of opposition and set the tone for the remainder of the Falkland conflict.

Had Prime Minister Thatcher started her address with a timorous message of weakness instead of strength, the outcome of the conflict might have ended in tragedy instead of triumph.

First Impressions are Lasting Impressions

Your first 10 words are more important than your next 10,000.

—Elmer Wheeler

Although the saying, "You never get a second chance to make a first impression" is a bit of an exaggeration, it is true that the first few minutes of a presentation make an impression on the minds of participants. Because the introduction sets the tone for the remainder of the presentation, "Getting off on the right foot" is an important part of delivering a successful presentation.

The introduction is the perfect opportunity for presenters to start off with a punch. Because in the first few minutes of a presentation participants are alert, attentive, and focused on the presenter, presenters need to make the most of the opportunity.

When Meriwether Lewis and William Clark encountered the first tribe of Indians on their famed expedition (1803-1806), they did not know what to expect. They had been commissioned by President Thomas Jefferson to get to the Pacific and return with as much information as possible. Relations with the Indians were important, establishing commercial ties with the various tribes was desirable, but the *sine qua non* of the expedition was to find a navigable route to the Pacific Ocean. To achieve this objective, the Corps of Discovery did not take any chances. They were armed to the hilt—a floating arsenal with enough powder, weapons, and ammunitions to supply a small army. There was a cannon on the bow of the keelboat, and every man was equipped with rifle, ball, and powder.

On August 2, 1803, the party encountered the Otos, a tribe of Indians on the lower Missouri river. The captains invited them to a council the next day at their campsite, which they called Council Bluff (downriver from present day Council Bluffs, Iowa). The night was a restless one, marked by tension and anticipation instead of sleep.

In the morning, they met with the chiefs of the Oto tribe—the expedition's first, official meeting with Indians. Lewis ordered his men to dress in full military uniform and marched them in a close-order drill to show the Oto chiefs the discipline and capability of the Corps. This was the first time the Otos had seen men march in step, turn as if one, and fire a volley on command.

Lewis and Clark adorned themselves in full-dress uniform complete with swords, weaponry, and cocked hats. They knew that their appearance, demeanor, and choice of attire would affect the thinking and attitude of the Oto chiefs. They wanted to communicate a message of confidence and overwhelming military hegemony. It worked.

The next morning, Lewis and Clark were astonished when one of the Oto chiefs, Big Horse, showed up to their campsite completely naked. To emphasize his poverty, Big Horse stood in front of the captains entirely unclothed and explained that if they wanted peace with the Oto tribe, they would have to give whiskey and gifts to his people. Short on non-military supplies, and with a long journey in front of them, Lewis declined.

Dress the Part

The apparel oft proclaims the man.

—William Shakespeare

The encounter between Lewis and Clark and the Otos illustrates the power and influence of appearance and clothing (or the lack there of).

Lewis and Clark, dressed in full military garb communicated a message of strength, leadership, and preparedness. Their counterpart, Big Horse, communicated distress, destitution, and abject poverty.

All of us have been advised not to judge a book by its cover—but we all do it. The reality is that presenters are judged by the way they look. Like the Oto tribe evaluating Lewis and Clark, presentation participants are going to make immediate assessments based on the appearance of the presenter. Does the presenter look sharp, or does he look like his suit was just pulled out of some moth infested gym bag? Is this person dressed professionally or provocatively? You get the idea.

Like every other aspect of a presentation, dress and appearance either increase or decrease the influence of the presenter. If a presenter is dressed sloppily or looks unkempt, versus a competing presenter who is dressed professionally and looks sharp, power goes to the competitor.

Early in my sales career, I delivered a presentation to a committee of technicians. Because I anticipated that the audience would be dressed in casual attire, I chose to wear khaki pants and a corporate embroidered sweater. I was stunned when I entered the presentation room to find the committee members dressed in suits and ties. I felt foolish and uncomfortable and lacked a professional edge that every presenter desires. My choice of attire adversely affected my presentation.

Because dress and appearance influence communication, presenters should use dress and appearance to their advantage. That might mean dressing in a power suit for a formal presentation to a CEO. It might mean dressing semi-casually for an informal presentation with the floor manager of a manufacturing company. Just be sure to dress in a way that makes a good first impression and increases credibility.

When presentation attire is in question, the general rule is to dress up, not down. It is always easier to adjust clothing down than to adjust it up. For example, if a presenter arrives at a presentation in a suit and needs to dress down, he or she can always take off the jacket.

> **Caution!** Do not make the mistake of dressing more casually than your audience. Always err on the side of dressing up rather than dressing down.

Meet, Greet, and Relate

Whether making a presentation to an individual or committee, it is important to "meet, greet, and relate" to buyers with appropriate pleasantries and gestures.

When meeting with buyers, it's expected practice to shake hands firmly and say, "Good morning." "How are you?" "It's good to see you." "How has your day been going?" and so forth. Initial hand shakes and verbal pleasantries are an expected form of common courtesy and are indicative of a well-mannered individual who is aware of appropriate business etiquette.

For most salespeople, briefly mentioning subjects such as sports, the weather, or personal hobbies is an effective way to relate to a buyer and establish a point of common ground from which a conversation can be launched. In most cases, spending two or three minutes with pleasantries and small talk is sufficient to put participants at ease and establish a comfortable presentation environment.

I met with a group of business owners in Sydney, Australia. I happened to be in Australia during the Rugby World Cup and mentioned to the audience that, two nights prior, I had attended a semi-final game between England and France. As part of the pre-presentation small talk, I briefly mentioned that I had developed a fascination with the game of rugby. I was surprised by their response. Participants went from being somewhat distant and cold to being jovial and engaging. By simply mentioning my newly found interest in the game of rugby, the room erupted with applause. Consequently, I instructed our trainers to wear Australian rugby shirts for the rest of the trip!

The key is to tailor the style of the introduction to your clients. Some clients will want to get to know you before talking about business, others won't.

While engaged in small talk, some presenters are tempted to talk about controversial topics such as religion, politics, and sex. *Avoid this mistake.* People have an amazing amount of stored up energy (and sometimes frustration) with regard to social and political topics. Even casual remarks by a presenter can set off a powder keg response from buyers. Presenters are better off avoiding controversial subjects completely.

Character and Credibility

There are two primary purposes of an introduction in a sales presentation. The first is to build personal and corporate credibility. The second is to capture the attention of the audience.

Review the three primary characteristics of an effective presentation.

1. *Ethos (Character and Credibility)*
2. Pathos (Emotion and Delivery)
3. Logos (Logic and Content)

Strategic introductions address the *ethos* portion of the presentation and firmly establish personal and corporate credibility.

The Buyer Method

In order to fully grasp the importance of a good introduction, it helps to understand the mental and emotional process a buyer goes through in a sales presentation.

Buyers follow a consistent and predictable purchasing pattern, called the buyer method, when evaluating products and services. The buyer method represents the criteria buyers use before making a decision.[1]

Buyers consistently evaluate five criteria when deciding on a particular product or service, typically in a precise psychological order.

1. For an in-depth examination of the buyer method, see Chapter 6 in *Sales-Side Negotiation.*

The first evaluation buyers make is not about a product or service. It is about the salesperson. Outside of purchasing shelf products from retail stores, the first action buyers instinctively take is to size up the presenter.

Early in the presentation, buyers make quick assessments about the honesty, character, and experience of the presenter (ethos). Prospective buyers characteristically decide within the first few minutes of contact whether or not they trust the presenter enough to proceed to the next level of the selling process.

> **Note:** You validate your trustworthiness by who you are, not necessarily by what you say. The kind of person you are sends loud and clear signals to people. It is communicated on an intuitive level, but it is, nonetheless, communicated.

The Buyer Method

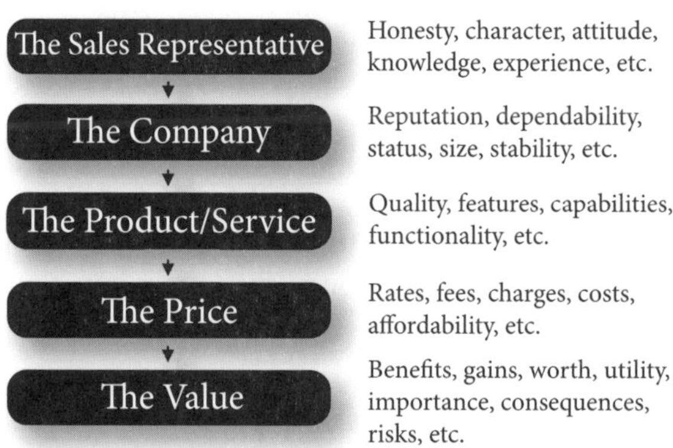

Figure 8.1

Five Questions Strategic Introductions Answer

The introduction is one of the few portions of the presentation in which presenters have the total focus and undivided attention of audience participants. Participants are very focused at the beginning of a presentation because they naturally experience "audience anxiety" in anticipation of the presentation. They have fundamental "who, what, when, why, and how" questions they want answered about the presenter, the topic, the timeframe, and the purpose of the presentation.

The five questions that audience participants instinctively want answered are:

1. Who are you?
2. When will you be through?
3. What are you going to talk about?
4. Why should I listen?
5. How are you going to make this interesting?

Strategic introductions answer these questions with five simple steps:

1. Introduce yourself (Who are you?)
2. Refer to a timeframe (When will you be through?)
3. Set the agenda (What are you going to talk about?)
4. Provide a corporate capabilities statement (Why should I listen?)
5. Quickly review client needs and pains (How are you going to make this interesting?)

> **Caution!** Although a strategic introduction answers multiple questions and fulfills a number of presentation objectives, it should not exceed fifteen minutes.

Step 1: Introduce Yourself

Introducing yourself gains audience attention and preemptively answers questions about who you are, which company you are with, your credentials, and the product you represent. There are certain personal, product, and corporate attributes and characteristics that audience members want to know, especially in a sales presentation: your name and title, the company or product you represent, where you are from , and your related experience and expertise.

Providing this information seems fundamental. Unfortunately, most presenters do a poor job of early identification and jump into the presentation without answering these important questions.

If a presenter has impressive credentials, he should not be shy about discussing them. A financial planner or insurance agent, for example, might begin a presentation by saying, "Before I begin, let me tell you a little about myself. First, following my degree in finance at UCLA and after receiving my MBA from Stanford, I began my career as an underwriter with John Hancock. I've been in business eleven years, and I am a member of the National Association of Underwriters. I've also been a member of my company's President's Club for the last seven years." By mentioning credentials, salespeople build credibility and communicate expertise in the represented field.

As important as introducing yourself is, there are presenters who take this principle to the extreme. There are things about the presenter that the audience does not want to know and that are not apropos to the presentation.

Winston Churchill once had a colleague in the British Parliament approach him and say, "You know, Sir Winston, I've never told you about my grandchildren." Churchill responded by clapping the man on the shoulder and saying, "I realize it, my dear fellow, and I can't tell you how grateful I am."

Many presenters believe that personal and family stories discussed in the introduction will personalize the presentation and warm up the audience. I have heard sales presenters start off presentations by introducing the names of family members, such as a son or daughter, and then sharing some experience related to that particular child. While these topics can be fun to talk about *for the presenter*, if they do not relate to the interests or business of the audience, they can potentially bore buyers, waste time, and squander the best opportunity to make a strong first impression.

This is not to say that briefly mentioning non-business related subjects can never be brought up in a presentation. Momentarily discussing these topics might be perfectly acceptable (and in some cases even preferable). Just don't overdo it. The introduction is too valuable to risk on topics that do not add to the substance of the presentation.

The Point? Small talk is good—in small doses. Big talk is better. Get down to business early in the presentation.

Step 2: Refer to the Timeframe

President William Henry Harrison was a man who did not have a good feel for presentation time-management. He delivered the longest inaugural address ever given. He broke the traditional inaugural timeframe by speaking outdoors for one hour and forty-five minutes. To make matters worse, it was delivered on a cold, rainy day in Washington D.C. As a result of his long winded speech, he developed pneumonia and died a few weeks later. Apparently, some observers said he deserved it.

Buyers typically provide a specific period of time for a seller to make a presentation. Participants want to know that the presenter is aware and committed to the allotted timeframe. Most presenters don't even mention timeframes until the end of the presentation when time is running out or when they realize they are going to go beyond the specified amount of time. The introduction, not the conclusion, is the appropriate time to communicate an awareness of the timeframe.

Communicate and confirm an awareness of time by posing a simple question to the audience: "I understand that we have until 11:00 A.M., is that right?" That simple question confirms two things: first, the allotted timeframe. Second, that you are aware of it.

Step 3: Set the Agenda

Setting the agenda provides audience participants with a clear snapshot of where the presentation is going. It supplies them with a mental map of both the direction and purpose of the presentation. For example, "Let me set the agenda. I am going to take a couple of minutes and introduce [the company]. Then we will review the [product or service] followed by a brief conclusion, and a short question/answer period."

By setting an agenda, presenters avoid potential disruptions. One can avoid, for example, a participant interrupting your presentation by asking questions such as, "When are you going to talk about X?" You can avoid participants getting up in the middle of a presentation to use the restroom because they are unaware of a scheduled break.

> **Note:** Setting the agenda follows the traditional presentation advice of, "Tell them what you're going to tell them. Tell them. Then tell them what you've told them."

Setting an agenda is important enough that many presenters provide agenda handouts prior to a presentation or review the agenda using PowerPoint. Regardless of what means you choose to use when setting an agenda, just be sure to do it.

Step 4: Provide a Corporate Capabilities Statement

The corporate capabilities statement is the heart of the introduction. It represents the strategic side of the introduction and provides participants with the intangible benefits offered by the represented business or corporation. The corporate capabilities statement introduces and summarizes the advantage of doing business with your company and includes three points of emphasis:

1. The company's background, stability, and reputation.
2. The company's experience and expertise (what the company does well in relation to other client relationships).

3. Intangible, indemonstrable benefits (customer service, technical support, etc.).

After buyers form a positive impression of the presenter, they evaluate the company. "Does the company have a good reputation?" "How long have they been in business?" "Will it back its commitments?" "Will it deliver as promised?" "Is it dependable?" "Is it financially stable?" The company's dependability, history, market position, financial stability, brand status, and service reputation all build or diminish power and credibility.

Back in the 1960's and 70's, IBM established a reputation as the epitome of corporate stability. To this day, IBM is commonly referred to as "Big Blue." Because of IBM's corporate reputation, buyers felt safe purchasing their goods and services. IBM played heavily on its corporate reputation and used it to intimidate competitors and sell products at higher prices. They perpetuated the pithy presentation slogan, "No one ever gets fired for going with IBM." Their corporate reputation gave them power.

Establishing a strong corporate image can also help with negotiation. When it comes time to negotiate the price of the presented product or service, your company reputation will be an ally or an enemy. If you have a reputation for outstanding service and high quality, buyers won't expect you to sell at prices on the same level as competitors with a reputation for poor service or low quality. If you establish a professional, reputable corporate image, buyers will be at a psychological disadvantage when negotiating purchasing terms. They will mentally expect to pay more and negotiate less.[2] Delivered appropriately, the corporate capabilities statement will establish corporate credibility and power.

Note: The stronger you position your company in the presenting process, the more power you will have in the negotiating process.

---

2. See Chapter 3 in *Sales-Side Negotiation.*

Corporate capabilities statements also project confidence. Confidence is the greatest indicator of a presenter's success. People who exude confidence instill confidence in others. When presenters show confidence in their company, it's noticeable. People recognize it. They sense it. They can feel by the presenter's words that he or she really believes in the company. By providing a corporate capabilities statement, presenters project certainty and eliminate doubt.

Keep in mind that corporate capabilities statements are not "brag" statements and should not sound arrogant. The purpose of the corporate capabilities statement is to imply value. The best (and quickest) way to imply value is to reference the value you have provided other clients. By referencing a success story, testimonial, or making a bold statement of achievement, you provide buyers a profile of the value you have offered other customers.[3]

> **Note:** Associating a corporate capabilities statement with a client reference or testimonial adds sting to the introduction.

Although important, corporate capabilities statements should not be long or elaborate. The purpose of the corporate capabilities statement is to add power to the introduction and give buyers a compelling reason to listen to the presentation. This can be accomplished with a *brief* but strategically delivered corporate capabilities statement.

Step 5: Quickly Review Client Needs and Pains

Many presenters find it helpful to conduct a quick needs analysis before delivering the bulk of the presentation. This provides presenters with an opportunity to either identify or review the primary buying motives of the attendees and match buyer needs to product or service solutions.

3. See Chapter 9 in *Power Prospecting* to learn how to effectively reference a success story or make a bold statement of achievement.

Sample Corporate Capabilities Statement

The following is a corporate capabilities statement *Patrick Henry & Associates,* created for a team of sales professionals who sell technical and networking solutions. For privacy reasons, the referenced names have been excluded. After introducing him or herself, referencing the timeframe, and setting an agenda, the presenter would say:

"Let me take a few minutes and talk briefly about X corporation. We have been in business for 12 years. We are debt free, financially strong, and have one of the largest research and development budgets in the industry. We have an installed base of over 10,000 sites and currently have customers in over 40 countries. Our founder, John Smith, saw a need for a cross platform networking solution that allowed both Windows and Macintosh platforms to communicate with each other over a single network. For that reason, we are both a certified Microsoft solutions provider and an Apple developer. [Company background, stability, experience, and expertise].

There are two primary reasons our product is consistently and overwhelmingly chosen. The first is our unique software and networking solutions, which I will demonstrate throughout the presentation. The second is our superior technical and customer support. We have the happiest customers and the best reputation for customer service in the industry. (The following is a handout that was printed off of an Internet "listserv" submitted by actual users comparing the customer service of major providers in the industry. As you can see, we have an ecstatic customer base). [Corporate reputation].

Our customer support is the best in the industry for three primary reasons:

1. We are the only company that provides 24 hours, 7 days a week technical support.
2. We are the only company that provides pro-active customer courtesy calls twice a year.
3. We are the only company that provides free upgrades (as long as customers are current with their support subscription).

All of these services are totally unique in the industry and exclusive to our company. [Intangible, indemonstrable benefits].

Enough about us, let's talk about your organization. [Transition statement] As you look at your networking challenges, what are your most important needs? [Quickly review client needs and pains]."

Figure 8.2

I delivered a presentation to a group of technicians in which the needs analysis revealed some gaping holes in their existing technical infrastructure. As I began asking need-problem questions, a flood of issues surfaced that I wrote in big, bold type on a whiteboard. After I had identified their main problems, I then began to systematically demonstrate how our product solved their problems. As a solution for each problem was presented, I would visually check off the identified problem as being addressed or solved. It worked fabulously. At the conclusion of the presentation, the committee verbally committed to the sale. I was stunned. This was a big sale, involved multiple competitors, and I was expecting a three to six month sales cycle. I am convinced it was the needs analysis that won that sale. Instead of delivering a traditional "show up, throw up" presentation, I took the time to diagnose and really understand their technical problems and system bottlenecks. Apparently, my competitors did not.

By reviewing critical needs and existing problems at the beginning of the presentation, presenters provide participants with an opportunity to help establish the direction of the presentation. By encouraging buyers to reiterate or articulate existing needs and problems, participants develop a sense of ownership in the presentation. Of course, when participants feel a sense of ownership in defining the problems, they are more easily persuaded to purchase the solutions.

The easiest and most effective way to conduct a needs analysis is to ask need-problem questions (see Chapter 4). For example, presenters might start off the needs analysis by asking, "As you look at this project, what are your most important needs?" Or, "What are some the most critical problems you are currently facing?" Presenters should then write the needs down on a whiteboard, chalkboard, or flip chart, and address them head-on during the presentation. By writing the needs and problems on a whiteboard or flipchart, presenters provide participants with a visible "needs list" to reference throughout the presentation.

When delivering a presentation to an individual or couple, write the needs down on a yellow pad of paper and then reference the needs during the presentation. An insurance agent might reference his notes and say, "Ms. Jones, earlier you mentioned how important maternity coverage is to you. Let me take just a minute and talk to you about our maternity plan."

In a large group setting, conducting a needs-analysis can be risky and lead to inter-participant discussions (that exclude the presenter), sometimes even inter-department arguments. *The risk associated with conducting a needs-analysis in a large group is losing control. To avoid this situation, make every effort to determine needs prior to the solution presentation.*

> **The Point?** The presentation agenda should be the agenda of the attendees and based on their needs, issues, and interests.

Creative Ideas for Introductions

In many cases, especially in committee-based presentations, it is perfectly acceptable to start off with a compelling fact, story, statistic, quote, historic event, or question. Immediately opening a presentation with a clever or creative introduction is called a "grabber." The opening words grab the attention of the audience.

Examples of effective grabbers include:

Quotations: Quotations are effective presentation openings for several reasons. First, they are easy to find and easy to relate to the presentation topic. Second, they make a presenter sound intelligent, thus enhancing credibility and making the presenter look prepared.

Humor: People like to laugh and, more importantly, like people who make them laugh. Humor is a great way to break the ice, build rapport, neutralize account opponents, and let participants see the presenter's human side. Presenters who can tell an appropriate joke or use humor effectively have a powerful presentation skill at their disposal.

Historic Events: Referencing a historical event that relates to the presentation topic will not only pique the interest of the audience, but will also make the presenter look educated, intelligent, and prepared.

Dates and Times: Facts about the date of the presentation can be extremely interesting. Stating that, "One hundred and fifty years ago today, Abraham Lincoln delivered the Gettysburg Address," will grab the attention of buyers. Quoting dates and times can have the same effect as using quotations or referencing historic events.

Rhetorical Questions: Asking a rhetorical question is an effective way to introduce a topic and gain the attention of an audience. For example, a person selling Internet based products or services might say, "Why are over five million businesses accepting orders over the Internet?" Or, "Why are more and more businesses flocking to the Internet to sell their goods and services?"

Stories: Brief stories are wonderful presentation tools. Everyone loves a good story, especially if the stories are personal and relevant. Stories grab the attention of buyers and, used appropriately, can drive home important presentation points.

The Shocker: Some presenters use dramatic illustrations to gain the attention of buyers. For instance, a presenter selling safety equipment might display a pair of shattered safety glasses and state, "These glasses not only saved a person's vision, they also saved a manufacturer like you a multi-million dollar lawsuit."

> **Note:** Creative introductions do not replace the recommended five-step strategic introduction. Instead, they are used just prior to or just after the five-step introduction.

Regardless of the method or material a presenter uses to make an opening statement, the desired result is always the same—to make a positive, powerful impression. When developing an opening statement, be creative. Be fun. Be dynamic. Make a powerful first impression with an exciting, interesting, and upbeat introduction.

Introductions to Avoid

Because the first few minutes will set the tone for the remainder of the presentation, certain opening statements should be completely avoided;

The Bore: The biggest mistake a presenter can make during the introduction of a presentation is to sound monotone, boring, or lackluster. Presenters should take every precaution to be positive, energetic, and enthusiastic. Boring introductions lead to boring presentations. Enthusiastic introductions lead to enthusiastic buyers. (See Chapter 11).

The Apology: Do not begin a presentation by apologizing. Even if there is a reason to apologize, such as being unprepared, don't admit it. Apologetic opening statements discredit presenters and can come across as insulting to participants who took the time to show up to the presentation.

Inappropriate Humor: Bad jokes and distasteful humor should be avoided at all costs. There is nothing worse in a presentation environment than having a presenter make a sexist or racist remark, or "bomb" a joke. Not only is it uncomfortable for the presenter, it is also uncomfortable for the audience. Jokes should be reviewed and tested with friends and family before being used in a presentation.

In Summary

Well-planned introductions significantly enhance sales presentations. When you create and organize a presentation, be sure to include the five steps of the strategic introduction:

- Introduce yourself
- Refer to a timeframe
- Set an agenda
- Provide a corporate capabilities statement
- Quickly review client needs.

By implementing these five steps, presenters cover all the bases of an effective introduction.

Chapter 9

Compelling Messages

A speech has two parts. You must state your case, and you must prove it.

—Aristotle

Oratorical power does not arise from passionate declamation only. On November 19, 1863, Abraham Lincoln demonstrated the equal power of using simple, yet eloquent words, quietly spoken, to convey a message.

In the small town of Gettysburg, Pennsylvania, in July of 1863, Union and Confederate forces clashed in a battle that brought enormous casualties. In three days of hard fighting, the Union army suffered over 23,000 casualties, the Confederate army 28,000. However, there was no question that the Confederate army had suffered the greater blow.

Later that year, a Gettysburg attorney conceived the idea of dedicating a portion of the battlefield to become a National Soldiers' Cemetery. Although President Lincoln was invited to speak, the main address was delivered by the former President of Harvard, and noted orator, Edward Everett. Everett spoke to a crowd of close to 20,000 people for over two hours. At the conclusion of Everett's address, Abraham Lincoln rose to deliver a few remarks.

> Four score and seven years ago, our fathers brought forth on this continent, a new nation, conceived in liberty, and dedicated to the proposition that all men are created equal.
>
> Now we are engaged in a great civil war testing whether that nation, or any nation, so conceived and dedicated, can long endure. We are met on a great battlefield of that war. We have come to dedicate a portion of that field, as a final resting place for those who here gave their lives that

that nation might live. It is altogether fitting and proper that we should do this.

But in a larger sense we cannot dedicate—we cannot consecrate—we cannot hallow—this ground. The brave men, living and dead, who struggled here, have consecrated it, far above our poor power to add or detract. The world will little note, nor long remember what we say here, but it can never forget what they did here. It is for us the living, rather, to be dedicated here to the unfinished work which they who fought here have thus far so nobly advanced. It is rather for us to be here dedicated to the great task remaining before us—that from these honored dead we take increased devotion to that cause for which they gave the last full measure of devotion—that we here highly resolve that these dead shall not have died in vain—that this nation, under God, shall have a new birth of freedom—and that the government of the people, by the people, for the people shall not perish from the earth.[1]

Apart from the Sermon on the Mount, no speech has been so heavily analyzed by scholars. Abraham Lincoln spoke only 272 words in his Gettysburg address. Yet in his ten sentences, he delivered one of history's most memorable orations.

What is it about his address that is so fascinating to historians? Why are these ten sentences so mesmerizing to politicians, and why have students of oratory been studying this address since its inception? The reason? Its message. It is the message of the speech that is captivating. Abraham Lincoln was able to couch in a three-minute address a message of timeless importance.

---

1. John Grafton, *Abraham Lincoln Great Speeches* (New York: Dover Publications, 1991) 103.

In simple, yet penetrating language, he articulated the struggle for human freedom, hope, and responsibility.

Although Lincoln himself considered his speech to be a failure, it turned out to be one of history's most eloquent moments.

Compelling Messages: Logic and Content

The Gettysburg Address contains all of the elements of a successful presentation and is a blueprint for sales and non-sales presentations alike. Like all successful presentations, it contains a strong introduction, powerful content, and memorable conclusion.

In his farewell address on January 11th, 1989, President Ronald Reagan said, "I won a nickname: 'The Great Communicator.' But I never thought it was my style or the words I used that made a difference. It was the content. I wasn't a great communicator, but I did communicate great things." Obviously, creating substantive content is an essential part of preparing and delivering a successful presentation.

Take a moment and review the three characteristics of a successful presentation:

1. Ethos (Character and Credibility)
2. Pathos (Emotion and Delivery)
3. *Logos (Logic and Content)*

The body of a presentation deals with *logos*, the logic and content of a message. Logos has to do with the substance and rationale of a presentation. It is the overriding message and provides the details and reasons buyers should procure the presented product or service.

The body of a presentation provides supporting evidence and demonstrates the qualities of the proposed good or service. Without providing clear and compelling reasons to acquire products or services, participants are left with little or no incentive to take action.

Because most buyers make purchases based on emotions that are then justified with logic, providing logic is extremely important.

Although the introduction and delivery of the presentation provide emotional validation, it is the body of the presentation that provides the rationale to support a buying decision.

When people purchase a home, for example, they initially make a decision based on emotional attachment (pathos). "It looks beautiful." "It feels like our home." "I just love the Victorian look." It's only after buyers feel an emotional attachment that they begin to justify their decision with reason and logic (logos). "After all, this home will be an excellent investment." "Property values are going up." "Interest rates are at an all time low." "The school district in this area is excellent."

The Point? By providing buyers with information to support the value of the product or service, presenters fulfill a buyer's intellectual need to justify an emotional decision. Appeal to the reason of prospects with logical, content-rich messages.

Pain and Problem Resolution: Your Central Sales Message

The most intense emotion buyers experience is pain. Pain is such an intense feeling that people will do almost anything to eliminate it. People take action to avoid, prevent, or overcome pain faster than anything else they do in their lives.

The primary reason people buy is to reduce or eliminate pain—physical, mental, emotional, financial, social, even spiritual. *Eliminating pain and resolving problems is the primary motivating factor in any sale.* Think of anything you recently purchased. Was it not to eliminate some dissatisfaction, displeasure, or frustration?

I remodeled my home. As part of the remodeling project, I replaced all of the carpet on my entry-level floor with a hardwood floor. The reason isn't that I don't like the feel of carpet under my feet. It is because carpet attracts and retains dust more than hardwood, and I suffer from dust related allergies. I spent thousands of dollars on a hardwood floor to eliminate pain.

In business-to-business presentations, different members of an organization attend presentations for various reasons—in other words, because they experience diverse pains. A CEO's ultimate pain might be declining stock price. The VP of Finance might attend because profits are down. The VP of Marketing might attend because of customer erosion. The VP of Sales might attend because his sales staff is not meeting revenue expectations. The VP of Manufacturing might attend because manufacturing costs are up. Each member of a business organization experiences pains and problems that they would like to eliminate.

Even in non-corporate related sales, people primarily make purchases to eliminate pain. For example, people often buy new cars, not out of necessity, but for social reasons. Maybe their neighbor recently pulled up in a new BMW, and they don't want to be seen driving their Chevy Cavalier. Maybe they feel inferior or inadequate without driving the nicest car in the neighborhood. Maybe their current car embarrasses them. Each of these "pains" is addressed with the purchase of a new car.

In our corporate trainings, I am occasionally challenged by participants who ask, "Not all purchases are driven by pain, are they? What about luxury items? For example, what pains are resolved with the purchase of a yacht? People don't buy yachts because they have to. They buy them because they want to." While the premise of this challenge is correct, the conclusion is not. I typically respond to this question by asking, "Do people ever want something so much that not having it causes pain?" The answer is, "Of course." Sometimes the "desire to acquire," the yearning to possess, or the craving to experience something becomes the pain, i.e., the motivating factor that drives the sale.

Most major purchases can be traced to eliminating pain. In fact, without pain, there is probably no basis for a purchase in the first place. A customer who feels totally satisfied doesn't need a presenter's product or service.

Note: The formula is simple: P (N) = A. Pain leads to needs. Needs lead to action. Put another way, No pain = No change. Potential buyers will not change unless the pain of staying the same is greater than the pain of change.

Ultimately, products and services are evaluated in terms of pain and problem resolution. This is why addressing buyer pains and problems should be the central message of the presentation. This is also why *The DNASelling Method* is such an intrinsic part of the presentation process (see Chapters 3 and 4). By using need-problem and ascertain-pain questions, sellers unearth the pains and problems buyers are experiencing. Those issues can then be converted into presentation points and an overall presentation message. Without a comprehensive understanding of the buyer's needs, pains, and problems, sales professionals are left to create presentation messages without accurate, substantive, or compelling data.

Training participants frequently ask what the difference is between problems and pains. There is a critical, fundamental difference. Problems are described in logical, cognitive terms such as, "My computer is broken." Pains, on the other hand, are described in fervent, emotional terms such as, "It is extremely frustrating having to work late because of computer failures." When buyers use emotional words such as frustrated, upset, disappointed, irritated, concerned, worried, etc, you know you have hit the "pain vein." *Pain is the consequence or outcome of the problem.*[2]

> **The Point?** Make pain and problem resolution the central theme of your sales presentation.

Competitive Differential Advantages

Where there is no difference, there is only indifference.

—Louis Nizer

2. See Chapter 8 in *The DNASelling Method* for more information about identifying and distinguishing pains and problems.

Born in Pall Mall, Tennessee, Alvin York spent his younger years in the backwoods of Tennessee hunting and fishing. His fundamentalist Christian religion taught him to disapprove of killing in war, but he resolved his doubts after being inducted into the army in 1917. In France on October 8, 1918, York led a small unit against a much larger German machine gun detachment. Using a flanking maneuver, Sergeant York single-handedly charged the German line. Firing his rifle 17 times, he killed 17 Germans. Out of bullets, he killed 8 more Germans with his pistol. He secured a stronghold at the end of the German line, cut off any chance for retreat, and induced 132 Germans to surrender. His flanking strategy and expert marksmanship made him the greatest American hero of World War I, and earned him the Congressional Medal of Honor.

Outthinking, outmaneuvering, and outflanking an enemy is the pinnacle of military success, especially when facing overwhelming odds. Flanking strategies in the military are based on the principle of focusing *strength against weakness*. The same can be said in sales. Successful sellers focus presentations on their strengths and the competitor's weaknesses.

The primary objective of a sales presentation is to convince buyers that your product or service will address and resolve the needs, pains, and problems they are experiencing. However, there is an equally important purpose, and that is to demonstrate that your product or service will do it better than your competitor's. Winning presenters know that some basis of favorable differentiation is imperative to delivering a successful presentation.

Because most sales presentations involve competitors, presenters should outflank their opponents by focusing on unique and exclusive product or service benefits and hammer on competitive advantages that hone in on competitor weaknesses. (See Chapter 13 to learn how to "Slam competition with grace").

Unfortunately, traditional sales presenters lack the "will and skill" to effectively address competitor vulnerabilities. In many presentations, the only thing setting sellers apart is the company name on the business card. Winning presenters don't have this problem. They insert unique selling propositions (exclusive features and capabilities) and the strongest competitive strengths possible into their presentations. They make clear and definitive capability differentiations and use the magic words "unique," "only," and "exclusive." For example, "We are the *only* supplier that provides this service." "This is a benefit provided *exclusively* by X product." "Our twenty-four hours, seven days a week technical support is completely u*nique* within the industry."

Strong points and areas of excellence should be highlighted and emphasized to convince buyers that your product or service is superior. It is here that the *Presentation Pedigree* proves so powerful. It helps identify competitive advantages that can be strategically placed in the presentation outline and then articulated in the actual presentation.

Categories of differentiation include:

Product Uniqueness: features, functionality, and benefits exclusive to the represented product or company.

Distribution: distributing goods and services in ways that offer advantages over competitors (Dell Computer, Mary Kay, and Amazon.com are examples of using distribution as a differentiator.)

Customer Service: providing prompt attention, timely responses, after hour services, expert assistance, and a friendly staff (Southwest Airlines and Ritz Carlton Hotels are examples of using customer service as a differentiator.)

Specialization: providing goods and services that cater to a specific segment of a market (Apple Computer uses specialization as a differentiator by catering to the printing, graphic design, and film industries.)

Market Dominance: utilizing brand name recognition, accessibility, performance capacity, and market-place muscle as differentiators (Microsoft, Intel, and Wal-Mart are examples of market dominance differentiators.)

Competitive differentiation is what separates sales wins from sales losses. If buyers see products as essentially interchangeable, they will make purchasing decisions based solely on price. This is why winning presenters do more than affably communicate the features and functionality of their good or service. Instead, they focus on differentiations that emphasize unique selling points and competitive differential advantages.

> **The Point?** Present exclusive features and benefits. Don't waste time on basics. Highlight the differences between what you *can* do and what your competitor *cannot* do.

Conviction Requires Proof: The Power of Demonstrations, Testimonials, and Logic

A pharmaceutical salesperson who sells sleeping pills once related a humorous experience that illustrates the power of "proof." Midway through a presentation to a group of physicians, one of the attendees fell asleep and began snoring. The pharmaceutical salesperson stopped the presentation and woke the sleeping physician. Without hesitation, the physician stood up and said, "This drug has some real promise!"

In order to persuade buyers to make a purchase, they must first be convinced of the value of the proposed product or service. Like a court of law, conviction requires proof. Buyers want hard evidence to confirm and substantiate claimed product or service benefits.

There are three types of proof that can be used in a sales presentation:

1. Demonstrations
2. Testimonials
3. Logical Argument

Demonstrations

According to Stephen E. Ambrose, author of *Undaunted Courage*, Meriwether Lewis and William Clark "were advance men and traveling salesmen, in short, representing American business and the American people."[3] As representatives of American commerce, the captains sought to impress upon the native tribes the superior weaponry, merchandise, and products that would be made available if the tribes would submit to the terms of their "new father," Thomas Jefferson. As a means of defense, and to demonstrate the advanced capabilities of American weaponry, the captains equipped the expedition with the finest military equipment available, including a bow swivel gun. This small cannon could shoot buck shot, chains, and nails with amazing power and accuracy.

As the expedition proceeded up the Missouri river, they visited various tribes and attempted to establish political, diplomatic and trade relationships with the tribal chiefs. After a short council, the captains put on a traveling medical show. It started with a close-order drill by uniformed troops marching under the colors of the republic. After the drill, the captains displayed colorful blankets, a magnifying glass, and mirrors—items the natives had never seen before. Then they introduced the cannon. On Captain Lewis' signal, a detail fired three shots from the bow swivel gun. When the smoke cleared and the Indians recovered from their astonishment at the first cannon they had ever seen or heard, the captains distributed gifts to the chiefs that included knives, needles, razors, scissors, beads, tomahawks, and more.

Meriwether Lewis and William Clark understood the impact a live demonstration of their cannon would have on the Indians. Rather than verbally explain or *talk* about the military capabilities of the United States, they *demonstrated* those capabilities by allowing the tribal leaders to experience first-hand the power of their weaponry.

3. Stephen E. Ambrose, *Undaunted Courage* (New York: Simon & Schuster, 1996) 157.

Like Lewis and Clark, highly successful presenters use live demonstrations to illustrate the qualities and benefits of their product or service. They *demonstrate* rather than *articulate* their message and include content that validates the benefits of the proposed product or service. For example, skilled technical presenters visually demonstrate how the proposed technology addresses identified needs and problems. Successful phone system salespeople conduct live demonstrations to validate product claims and capabilities. Experienced medical device representatives demonstrate the utility of the proposed device.

I know a salesperson who sells high quality computer and networking wires and cables. Because of the quality of his cables, his prices are higher than his competitors. Because of the extra expense involved, some of his clients periodically drop his product. When one of his larger clients discontinued using his product, he decided enough was enough and arranged a meeting to demonstrate the value of his wires and cables.

After admitting that his product was more expensive, he stated to the audience that it was important to compare apples to apples. He then held up one of his competitor's wires and put a lighter underneath it. The casing around the wire began to melt and in a few seconds was on fire. His audience was astounded. He then held the lighter under his wire and reminded them that his wiring was fireproof. He concluded his presentation by asking a simple question, "Ladies and gentlemen, which wire do you want in your walls and computers?" His client cancelled the order from his competitor.

As previously addressed, the best way to demonstrate the worth of a product or service is to use scenarios illustrating the value of the offering. Rarely, if ever, should a feature or capability be presented without a scenario. Scenarios help buyers visualize and quasi-experience the utility of the product or service. Inserting a feature into a scenario illustrates both the feature and the benefit. Using the situations and experiences of the attendees, presenters address the specific needs, pains, and problems that participants face.

The Point? Use live demonstrations and scenarios whenever possible to bring facts and information to life.

Testimonials

In our presentation trainings, I frequently ask participants, "How many of you provide buyers with testimonial letters to support the success of your products and services?" I am always amazed at how few hands go up. Yet, what better evidence can a presenter have than a statement by a satisfied customer? When we talk about providing *proof* to validate product or capability claims, what better proof can a presenter offer than a testimonial?

A testimonial is nothing more than a type of evidence. Like a court of law, witnesses are called to testify to the truthfulness of certain facts or disputed claims. Client testimonials serve the same purpose. They illustrate how the proposed product or company has benefited other companies and organizations. Used appropriately, testimonials communicate similar benefits available to the targeted audience.

Because service oriented businesses cannot physically demonstrate the benefits they offer, it is especially important that service related presentations provide testimonials from existing clients to validate the claimed capabilities or benefits. Testimonials help substantiate benefits such as friendly customer service, excellent technical support, and on-time deliveries.

Logical Argument

All sales presentations should provide logic and rationale to support product or service capability claims. An R.O.I. (return on investment) sheet is a logical argument. I regularly use R.O.I. sheets to demonstrate the value of sales training. By calculating an estimated percent of increase in sales, multiplying it by the company's total sales, and subtracting the cost of the training, I provide buyers with an accurate forecast of the financial return they will receive on their investment. When I provide hard numbers that demonstrate the value of our training, buyers are logically convinced to make the investment.

Other options include: examples, facts, exhibits, testimonials, and statistics.

By providing buyers with *proof* of the value of the presented product or service, they are more easily convinced of the need to make the purchase.

The Power of Storytelling

The best supporting evidence for a message is a credible, meaningful story. In the mid-1970's, Nobel Prize-winning psychologist Daniel Kahneman and fellow researcher Amos Tversky demonstrated in their ground breaking research on behavioral economics that vivid stories and examples are overwhelmingly more influential in shaping decisions and opinions than abstract information.

The power of a well-delivered story in a presentation setting would be difficult to exaggerate. Similar to scenario selling, stories are captivating, entertaining, and memorable. Human beings have an innate interest in stories and yearn for information packed into this age-old communication format. Rooted deep in the human psyche is a natural interest in stories that involve other human beings.

In my early twenties, I spent two years on a voluntary mission in Southern Africa. I worked, visited, and lived in South Africa, Botswana, Lesotho, and Swaziland. I met incredibly interesting people and had extraordinary experiences.

While living in Johannesburg, I met a prominent South African businessman who was born and raised on the island of Tasmania, a former penal colony for Great Britain located off the southern coast of Australia. He was a self-made millionaire who later immigrated to South Africa. I once asked this man the secret of his success. Rather than rattle off five or six keys to success, he related a story to me.

His family had resided in a remote area of Tasmania and had lived by subsistence farming and hunting. As a young man, he went hunting with a boyhood friend. They were sitting down, resting on what appeared to be solid ground. In reality, they were sitting on solid brush. The brush was so thick that they could actually walk on it. While resting, an extremely venomous snake bit his friend on the thumb. His friend quickly reached over with the palm of his free hand and squeezed his lower thumb to stop the venom from circulating throughout the rest of his body. He then instructed his hunting partner (the man relating the story to me) to shoot his thumb off. Without hesitation, he picked up his shotgun, placed it against his friend's thumb and pulled the trigger.

I listened to his story in stunned disbelief. When he finished his story, he said to me in a strong Australian accent, "Young bloke, the will to survive is the most fundamental of all human instincts. Use it."

Nothing my Australian friend could have said would have had more of an impact on me than this story. His story was so vivid and so intense, that I still have a mental image of the look on his face when he related his experience to me. I remember where I was, what time of day it was, even the weather. His story engulfed me.

Using stories in a presentation goes beyond entertaining an audience. Stories also help with retention. People remember stories more than they do charts, graphs, or statistics. Think of your freshman year in high school. What is it that you remember? Is it the curriculum you learned in the classroom, or is it the stories about fire alarms, prom nights, and football games?

Storytelling is powerful because it touches both the logical and emotional sides of people. Stories not only make a point, they also reach the feelings and passions of participants. Stories can verbally paint a picture, drive home a point, or illustrate a problem with feeling and imagery.

I had an atheist call my radio talk show program and question my belief in God. He respected my political opinions but could not understand why an informed person acquainted with science would believe in "primitive religious superstitions." He then pressed me to prove the existence of God. I answered his question with a story.

"A medical student dissected a cadaver and commented to his professor, 'I opened every organ of the body and found no soul, so how can religious people say a soul exists?' The professor thoughtfully replied, 'When you opened the brain did you find an idea?' 'No,' replied the student. 'When you cut open the heart, did you find love?' 'No,' replied the student. 'When you dissected the eye, did you find vision?' 'No," replied the student. 'The professor then said, 'Because some things are not seen or proven does not mean they do not exist.'"

Months later, a listener to my radio program stopped me at a local sporting event and mentioned how impressed he was by that story. I could have argued and debated the existence of God until I was blue in the face, but nothing would have reached that listener like that particular story.

Storytelling is a great communication tool because people understand, enjoy, and remember stories more than they do facts and figures. There is nothing more enjoyable in a presentation setting than listening to a good story. Graphs, charts, statistics, and even witty one-liners are wonderful presentation tools. However, they pale in comparison to a well-timed, well-delivered story.

The Point? The best supporting evidence for a message is a credible, meaningful story.

Key Transitional Phrases

Winning presenters provide participants with clear presentation transitions called *key transitional phrases*. Key transitional phrases provide audience members with recognizable breaks between major points of discussion.

Because confused prospects don't buy, it's a good idea to provide participants with a clear understanding of where they are in relation to the presentation. Clear breaks between major points of discussion prevent buyers from blending or confusing presentation topics. Transitions serve to make clear distinctions between presentation topics and ensure that prospects do not get lost or confused. They signal to an audience that the presentation is about to address another topic, make a summary, or conclude. Transitions help ideas flow logically, introduce new subjects, and make clear links between old and new ideas. They also add clarity and help with topic comprehension and content retention.

Examples of transitions include:

"Enough about us. Let's dive into the software..."

"We have demonstrated how ABC feature can streamline the ordering process, now let's look at..."

"That concludes our demonstration of ABC capability. Let's talk now about customer service."

"We have seen how presentation training can increase sales revenue, let's switch gears and talk about how negotiation training can help increase sales margins."

"We have addressed the primary benefits associated with X product, let's conclude by reviewing..."

A key transitional phrase can also be used to emphasize the benefits of a product or service. For example, after demonstrating the capabilities of a good or service, a presenter might use transitional words and phrases such as, "thus," "therefore," "which means," "so," "which provides," or "as a result," to transition audience attention from the features of the solution to the benefits of the solution (see Chapter 12).

The Point? Use key transitional phrases to keep presentation topics clear and understandable.

Be Concise

Excellent presentations get to the point, never dragging out or elongating a point unnecessarily. As Abraham Lincoln demonstrated, a concise message can be extremely powerful. Consider that his Gettysburg Address is just 272 words in length. Out of those 272 words, 185 have only one syllable. The story of creation is told in the book of Genesis in 400 words. The Ten Commandments contain only 297 words. The United States *Declaration of Independence* required only 1,432 words. Keep your presentation as concise as possible.

In Summary

Because people buy emotionally and justify decisions logically, it is important to supply rationale to justify purchasing decisions. The message of the sales presentation provides just that—evidence. It demonstrates how the proposed product or service eliminates pains and problems and establishes clear, competitive advantages. It uses stories and scenarios to convince buyers of the need for the proposed product or service. In other words, the body of the sales message provides buyers with compelling reasons to purchase the presented product or service.

Chapter 10

Memorable Conclusions

It is by entrances and exits shall ye be known.

—Shakespeare

In 1588, Spain was a vast empire. Since the glory days of Rome, no country had been able to boast of more territory than Spain. Spain controlled much of Europe, North Africa, parts of Asia, and most of Latin America. Spain was a glorious spectacle of an empire—a colossal power.

Pitted against this enormous empire was feeble little England. In 1588, England was a tiny country, strong in courage and ambition, but weak in territory, allies, and military strength. With the exception of the Dutch, England had no foreign power as an ally. Scotland was a separate kingdom, and Ireland was in the throes of revolt. It was David against Goliath—a tiny island defying a world empire.

Spain was ruled by Phillip II, a fervent Catholic and leader of the Counter Reformation. He hated Protestants, especially English Protestants, and authorized the burning of heretics in a ceremony called *acto-de-fe* (act of faith).

Enmity between the two countries had been building up to a climax. Tired of English raids on Spanish commerce, and eager to convert England to Catholicism, Phillip II sent a powerful armada to conquer England, consisting of over 130 ships and carrying an army of close to 20,000 soldiers.

Against this Spanish assault stood one of history's shrewdest leaders—Queen Elizabeth I of England, daughter of Henry VIII and Ann Boleyn.

Queen Elizabeth was not a warlike leader and preferred diplomacy to the force of arms. Threatened with invasion, however, she rose to heights of eloquence that would not be equaled until the World War II leadership of Winston Churchill.

As the Spanish Armada approached the shores of England, Queen Elizabeth went to Tilbury to examine her troops and stiffen morale. Mounted on a fine white horse, she watched a mock battle and then addressed her soldiers. After delivering a rousing speech, she concluded with a paragraph that contains her now famous quote, "I have the heart and stomach of a King."

> I know I have the body of a weak and feeble woman, but I have the heart and stomach of a king, and of a King of England too, and think foul scorn that Parma or Spain or any Prince of Europe should dare to invade the borders of my realm, to which, rather than any dishonor shall grow by me, I myself will take up arms, I myself will be your general, judge and rewarder of every one of your virtues in the field… By your valour in the field, we shall shortly have a famous victory over these enemies of my God, of my kingdom, and of my people.

Queen Elizabeth's speech transformed threat into national strength and crisis into triumph. Although the British Royal Navy numbered only 39 ships, Queen Elizabeth armed her troops with something much more powerful than galleys and guns. She armed them with a spirit and determination of an unconquerable people, a spirit and determination personified in her reign as queen of England.

While still in Tilbury, Queen Elizabeth received news that the invincible Spanish Armada had been crushed. Equipped with smaller, more versatile ships, and armed with an almost reckless confidence, Sir Francis Drake and his English "sea dogs" repulsed one of the largest maritime invasions in history.

Memorable Conclusions: The Law of Recency

Queen Elizabeth's "Stomach of a King" speech is a classic example of ending a presentation with a strong and memorable conclusion.

Strong conclusions are not only motivational; they also impact the overall success of a presentation. Because the conclusion is what participants hear last, it is imperative to close the presentation with a powerful and memorable message. This is why planning a powerful conclusion is as important as planning a strong introduction.

Unfortunately, powerful conclusions are the most ignored aspect of sales presentations. Traditional conclusions do not leave powerful impressions, foster content retention, or give buyers any overpowering reason to buy.

Review the laws of memorable impact:

1. Law of Primacy: people remember what they hear first.
2. Law of Frequency: people remember what they hear most.
3. *Law of Recency: people remember what they hear last.*

Audience participants remember the beginning and the end of a presentation more than the middle. They also remember the end of a presentation more than the beginning. No matter how eloquent a presenter is in the opening and middle of a presentation, if the close is a clunker, that's what the audience will remember.

In October of 1957, Americans were shocked to learn that the Soviet Union had launched the world's first satellite. Named *Sputnik*, the 184-pound satellite orbited the earth every ninety minutes. A few weeks later, the Soviets stunned Americans again by launching a second satellite, but this time there was a dramatic twist. The satellite would contain the world's first space traveler—a dog named Laika. Soviet radio announced that Laika would be riding in an air conditioned cockpit as she rocketed through space at eighteen thousand miles an hour.

Unfortunately for Laika, the Russians had no way of bringing her back. Three days into her space journey, oxygen ran out. A short time later, her satellite burned up after its orbit decayed, and it reentered the earth's atmosphere.

Worried about the technical advances of the Soviets, The United States government launched its own space program, NASA, to compete with the Russians. A space race was on, thanks in part to a dog nicknamed by Americans, *Muttnick*.

Planning Memorable Conclusions

Many sales presenters make the same mistake the Soviets made with Sputnik—they don't have an exit strategy. They fly off into orbit without planning a closing strategy.

I have often asked, "Why are powerful conclusions such a rarity in sales presentations?" I have concluded that there are numerous reasons: presenters are fatigued, stressed, shaken, pressured, running out of time, etc. I am convinced, however, that the number one reason most presenters deliver poor conclusions is due to poor planning—many presenters don't even plan a conclusion.

The purpose of the conclusion is identical to the purpose of the entire presentation: *impression*, *retention*, and *selection*. Unfortunately, the purpose of many conclusions is to let the audience know that it's time to wake up. Winning presenters don't have this problem. Their conclusions end with a bang. They are dramatic and memorable.

There are four steps to a memorable conclusion:

1. End on time
2. Summarize hot points and competitive differential advantages
3. Conclude with a compelling closing sentence
4. Transition to the closing stage of the sales cycle

Queen Elizabeth I had little tolerance for long-winded or loquacious speakers and was notoriously critical of long sermons. On one occasion, the dean of St. Paul's cathedral seriously tried her patience when he strayed into a tedious condemnation of the display of crucifixes and candles in private chapels. Elizabeth, polite in most other contexts, interrupted the cleric and said, "Do not talk about that. Leave that! Leave that! It has nothing to do with your subject, and the matter is threadbare."

Step 1: End on Time

Verbose presenters waste time, stray from the point or purpose of their presentation, and frustrate buyers. In business-to-business presentations especially, time is money. Business leaders understand that time is irreplaceable once lost and that it should not be squandered.

Although many presenters say, "I'll need about an hour" when setting up a presentation, they often break their timeframe agreement and continue presenting as if they never made the one-hour commitment in the first place. Not only is going over allotted time allowances discourteous, it is also unprofessional and can lessen the credibility of a presenter.

A frequently asked question I hear during presentation trainings is, "What happens if I need a little more time to make my point? Should I end my presentation or should I just keep going?" Great question—easy answer: get permission.

I delivered a presentation to a group of technicians in Portland, Maine. Because of audience questions and lack of timing on my part, I passed my allotted time. I began to panic because I had saved the best for last. Rather than requesting an extra fifteen minutes, I kept presenting. It backfired. About five minutes after my allotted timeframe had expired, the primary decision maker (a corporate level IT director) stood up and walked out. When he walked out of the room, it was a signal to the other attendees that he was annoyed because I had not honored our allotted timeframe. The feeling and ambiance in the room went from being encouraging to depressing. When he walked out of the room, it was as if all the positive energy walked out with him.

If presentation time is running out, ask for more time (no more than half an hour). Simply state to the audience, "I committed to finish my presentation within one hour, and it looks like my time is quickly coming to a close. Would it be acceptable for me to take an extra ten minutes and address a few very important points concerning ABC product?" If the request for additional time is denied, respect their decision and close on time. You will gain greater credibility by adhering to your timeframe commitment than you will by cramming in a few extra closing points.

The Point? Participants have a psychological need for closure—they don't want to be left hanging or asking themselves, "I wonder when this person is going to sit down?" Ending on time brings anticipated closure to a presentation.

Step 2: Summarize Hot Points and Competitive Differential Advantages

The most important part of the memorable conclusion is summarizing hot points and emphasizing competitive differential advantages. At the conclusion of a presentation, briefly and quickly review the highlights of the presentation with simple, bold, and to-the-point sentences, such as, "Earlier we discussed your need to provide suppliers with secured access to your documents. X product uses SSL encryption in its Web technology and provides suppliers with online support and immediate online assistance. This benefit is completely *unique* and *only* available from ABC Corporation."

Recapping information at the end of a presentation is an effective way to reinforce hot points and highlight competitive advantages.

Note: Product solutions and unique selling points can also be summarized at the conclusion of a presentation with handouts.

Step 3: Conclude with a Compelling Closing Sentence

Step three is providing buyers with a compelling closing sentence. This is the punch line. The compelling closing sentence summarizes the most important points of the presentation and pulls things together in one final sentence. The compelling sentence tells the audience in a single phrase why they should buy from you instead of from someone else. The compelling closing sentence is a great time to utilize "the rule of three" as addressed in Chapter 6.

Examples of compelling closing sentences include:

> "By implementing X training program, your sales staff will be better trained, more skilled, and capable of defeating even your strongest competitors."
>
> "As you can see, X product will streamline your manufacturing process, improve productivity, and increase profitability."
>
> "As demonstrated today, ABC corporation eliminates X problem, is the exclusive provider of Y capability, and provides the best customer support in the industry."

Effective conclusions are explicitly stated rather than left vague or unclear. The compelling closing sentence makes a final impression and provides buyers with convincing reasons to purchase the proposed solution.

> **Caution!** Highlighted points in the compelling closing sentence need to be limited to three (no more than five) and should be strategically designed and rehearsed prior to a presentation.

Creative Ideas for Conclusions

Like the introduction of a presentation, concluding remarks should be carefully considered to ensure maximum impact and retention (especially with large audiences or committee-based presentations). I learned the power of a good conclusion while speaking internationally with Brian Tracy, Dr. William Danko (co-author of *The New York Times* best seller, *The Millionaire Next Door*), and other reputable authors, motivators, and business leaders. When I started the tour, I made the traditional presentation mistake of not placing enough emphasis on my closing remarks. Although my presentations were successful, I sensed a lack of "oomph" and meaningful closure in my conclusions. My closing remarks didn't seem to have any sting. I decided to experiment with various closing methods to improve my presentation. I tested various poems, motivational quotes, and historical events that tied into the point of the presentation. All of them worked fantastically and my success ratios skyrocketed.

The key to powerful conclusions is creativity. Creative conclusions are motivating, captivating, and interesting. They are also memorable and fun. Examples of creative conclusions include:

Reciting a Poem: Poems are great closers, but they need to relate directly to the presentation topic, and they must be short. For example:

> I love a finished speaker.
> I really truly do.
> I don't mean one who's polished.
> I just mean one who's through.

Quotations: I regularly conclude my presentations with a motivational quote from Teddy Roosevelt. Quotations make good conclusions for several reasons. First, well-chosen quotations are motivating. Second, they can drive home a desired point—especially when quoting a known authority figure on a subject. Third, when memorized, they make presenters look educated and intelligent.[1]

---

1. Great resource for quotes on the Internet include: www.QuoteLand.com, www.QuoteWorld.com, www.QuoteGeek.com, www.Famous-Quotations.com, and www.QuotationsPage.com.

Historic Events: One of my favorite methods for concluding a presentation is referencing an historical event that relates to the presentation topic. Referencing an historical event can make a presenter look intelligent, cerebral, and, of course, historically knowledgeable—all of which builds credibility. The key to relating an interesting historical event is to keep it brief.

Humor: Humor is a great way to solidify likeability and make people feel comfortable about both presenters and products. People like to laugh and like people who make them laugh.

Stories: As previously discussed, stories are wonderful presentation tools. Everyone loves a good story, especially if it is personal and relevant to the topic at hand. Stories grab the attention of buyers and, used appropriately, can drive home an important presentation point. Brief, relevant stories make powerful conclusions.

Ronald Reagan was famous for using creative stories and humorous anecdotes to conclude his remarks. His sense of humor and communication skills earned him the nickname "The Great Communicator." During a presidential address on Labor Day, he concluded his speech with the following humorous story:

> It's like the fellow who took some land down by the creek bottom all covered with brush and rocks. And he cleared the brush and he hauled the rocks away. And then he started cultivating, and then he planted. And finally he had a beautiful garden. He was so proud that one Sunday after the church service he asked the minister if he wouldn't come by and see what he had done. So the minister came by, and when he saw the corn that had been planted there, he said he had never seen corn so tall, and the Lord had really blessed the land. And then he looked at the melons, and he said he'd never seen any as big as that, and thank the Lord for that. And he went on praising the Lord for everything—the

> squash and the beans and everything else. The farmer was getting a little fidgety. Finally, he interrupted and said, "Reverend, I wish you could have seen this place when the Lord was doing it all by himself."

Ronald Reagan used this story to make a point and subtly thank American farmers for all of the hard work they do.

Humorous stories and anecdotes are extraordinary presentation tools. Used appropriately, they can win over an audience faster than any other presentation skill I am aware of.

Step 4: Transition to the Closing Stage of the Sales Cycle

Following the compelling closing sentence, choose from the following key transitional statements to transition buyers to the closing stage of the sales cycle:

> "That wraps up the presentation. What's the next best step to move this project forward?"
>
> "That concludes the presentation. What benefits, if any, do you anticipate from implementing the proposed solutions?"
>
> "Based on what we've discussed, how do you see this service working for your company?"

Note: Summary questions psychologically prepare buyers to purchase.

Based on the criteria provided, it should be clear what benefits are available to the buyer. Presenters should capitalize this momentum by recommending a suggested course of action. "Based on your department's needs and financial considerations, I would suggest that implementing X version would be the best fit. What do you think?"

Many presenters are fearful of discussing solution costs following a sales presentation because of the risk of losing momentum. In many cases, this perception is incorrect. The perfect time to justify costs is immediately following a presentation when competitive differences and the value of the offer are fresh in the minds of buyers. Rather than avoid discussions about proposed product or service costs following a presentation, I recommend addressing them directly to transition buyers from the presentation stage of the sales cycle to the closing stage of the sales cycle.[2]

In some cases (especially in larger, more complex sales), discussing solution costs following a presentation is not optional or advisable. Because of time restraints, prior discussions, or scheduled proposal meetings, following a presentation with a cost discussion may not be appropriate.

At the conclusion of a presentation, prospects *should* be conversing about post sale matters such as delivery, support, terms and conditions, pricing structures, etc. If they are not, all indications are that the sale has not yet progressed to the closing stage of the sales cycle and that objections to making the purchase still need to be overcome.[3]

In Summary

Like introductions, the purpose of a conclusion is to recommend a specific course of action and make a powerful, lasting impression. When you create a conclusion, be creative. Be fun. Be dynamic. Be original. Do anything and everything to avoid being boring, lackluster, or monotonous. Add spice to your closing remarks to interest, excite, and motivate buyers to take action.

Be sure to end your presentation on time, summarize hot points and competitive differential advantages, and conclude with a compelling closing sentence to transition buyers from the presentation stage of the sales cycle to the closing stage.

---

2. See Chapter 20 in *The DNASelling Method* to learn effective closing strategies.

3. See Chapter 17 in *The DNASelling Method* for information regarding preventing and overcoming objections.

Winning Sales Presentation Framework

Introduction

- ➢ Introduce yourself: Name, Title, Experience & Expertise
- ➢ Refer to the Timeframe
- ➢ Set the Agenda
- ➢ Deliver a Corporate Capabilities Statement
    - Company Background
    - Company Experience & Expertise
    - Intangible Corporate Benefits
- ➢ (Optional) Quickly Review Client Needs, Pains, or Problems

<Key Transitional Phrase>

Content

A. Topic, Feature, Capability, Benefit, or Competitive Advantage
   1. Supporting Evidence
      i) Scenario, Story, Example, Demonstration, Testimonial
      ii) Scenario, Story, Example, Demonstration, Testimonial
         a. Topic Summary

<Key Transitional Phrase>

B. Topic, Feature, Capability, Benefit, or Competitive Advantage
   1. Supporting Evidence
      i) Scenario, Story, Example, Demonstration, Testimonial
      ii) Scenario, Story, Example, Demonstration, Testimonial
         a. Topic Summary

<Key Transitional Phrase>

Conclusion

- ➢ Summarize Hot Points and Competitive Differential Advantages
- ➢ Compelling Closing Sentence
- ➢ Transition to Close

Figure 10.1

III

part three

Presentation Delivery

Chapter 11

Presenting 101

Victory belongs to those who fight most passionately.

—Anonymous

In 1764, the British Empire was in desperate need of cash. Territorial expansion, colonialism, and wars with France had drained the empire's treasury. King George III was determined that the colonies in America should pay their share of the expenses for the empire, so through the British parliament, he passed a number of legislative acts such as the Molasses Act, Stamp Act, and Quartering Act to raise funds and cut costs. These acts restricted American trade, mandated burdensome tariffs on American goods, and imposed taxes without American representation.

Fed up with the arrogance of King George and the injustice of the British Parliament, revolutionaries such as Samuel Adams, Paul Revere, and John Hancock began challenging the constitutionality of King George's policies. Talk of separation and independence dominated the taverns of America. But not all Americans were in favor of independence. In the initial stages of the American Revolution, over half of the colonial citizens considered themselves loyal to the crown and defended the interests of the King. Even men who became prominent revolutionaries, such as Thomas Jefferson and George Washington, were at first, reluctant to join the *radicals* and openly defy King George.

In 1775, a Continental Congress was called to address the issue of independence. Following the Continental Congress, the state of Virginia held the Second Virginia Convention to vote on resolutions passed by the Continental Congress. Virginia was the most influential of the thirteen colonies and was the home of George Washington, James Madison, John Randolph, George Mason, John Marshal, and Thomas Jefferson. Delegates poured in from all over Virginia to attend the convention in St. John's church in Richmond. The convention was packed with both delegates and onlookers, many of whom were still undecided on the issue of independence.

One delegate of notice was a Virginian patriot and successful lawyer named Patrick Henry. Patrick Henry was a passionate advocate of American independence and a renowned orator. He submitted a litany of resolutions stating that a militia was the only security of a free people and was necessary to protect American rights and liberties. The powerful Loyalists, most notably Peyton Randolph, opposed his resolutions. Peyton Randolph was the former attorney for King George III and was the Speaker of the Virginia House.

As Patrick Henry took the floor to defend his resolutions, he was aware that his words could potentially cost him his life.

> Mr. President, it is natural to man to indulge in the illusions of hope. We are apt to shut our eyes against a painful truth, and listen to the song of that siren, till she transforms us into beasts. Is this the part of wise men, engaged in a great and arduous struggle for liberty?... judging by the past, I wish to know what there has been in the conduct of the British ministry for the last ten years, to justify those hopes with which gentlemen have been so pleased to solace themselves and the House? Is it that insidious smile with which our petition has been lately received? Trust it not, sir; it will prove a snare to your feet. Suffer not yourselves to be betrayed with a kiss... They tell us sir, that we are weak; unable to cope with so formidable an adversary. But when shall we be stronger? Will it be the next week, or the next year? Will it be when we are totally disarmed, and when a British guard shall be stationed in every house?... It is vain, sir, to extenuate the matter. Gentlemen may cry peace, peace—but there is no peace. The war has actually begun!... Our brethren are already in the

> field! Why stand we here idle? What is it that gentlemen wish? What would they have? Is life so dear, or peace so sweet, as to be purchased at the price of chains and slavery? Forbid it, Almighty God! I know not what course others may take; but as for me, give me liberty, or give me death!

Patrick Henry's electrifying declaration shattered the complacency and timid indecision of the Tory delegates. His utterance was a bold defiance of British misrule and an appeal directed to the hearts of men who loved Liberty. In the audience sat Mason, Jefferson, and Washington—future revolutionaries inspired by Henry's impassioned plea for independence.

Patrick Henry's "Liberty or Death" speech elevated revolutionary fervor to a fever pitch. His passion, energy, and oratory led Thomas Jefferson to call him "The leader of the revolution." The American Revolution was launched from this address and has become one of the most important and most recognized speeches in American history.

Pathos: The Emotion and Delivery of a Successful Presentation

Embedded in Patrick Henry's address are the elemental skills of presenting. His speech embodies all of the successful components of a presentation including a forceful introduction, powerful message, and unforgettable conclusion. Perhaps, though, the most important element of his speech was his delivery. Patrick Henry delivered his address with the most influential tool known to man: passion. Passion distinguished Patrick Henry's speech from other revolutionary orators. Passion moved his audience to action. Passion inspired his most important audience member, Thomas Jefferson, to choose independence. Passion led him to utter his now famous words, "Give me liberty, or give me death!" Passion made Patrick Henry one of the most gifted orators of the ages, and America's great awakener.

> **The Point?** Presentations executed passionately will always outperform competitive presentations executed non-passionately.

The Seven Categories of Good Delivery Skills

There are seven primary categories associated with good delivery skills:

1. Showing Passion and Enthusiasm
2. Being Positive and Optimistic
3. Communicating Confidence
4. Using Appropriate Humor
5. Never Panicking (The Crisis Creates Opportunity Theory)
6. Utilizing Appropriate Voice Inflection, Eye Contact, and Body Language
7. Using Effective Language

Of course, there are dozens of related delivery skills important to successful presentations, but all major delivery skills are either related to or could be considered sub-categories of the above seven skills.

Show Passion and Enthusiasm

As I previously addressed, there are three characteristics of a successful presentation.

1. Ethos (Character and Credibility)
2. *Pathos (Emotion and Delivery)*
3. Logos (Logic and Content)

The most important factor of a successful presentation is *pathos*: the emotion and delivery skills of the presenter. *Pathos* refers to the right brain, creative side of a presentation. It represents the passion, enthusiasm, and delivery skills of the presenter—skills that can reach the hearts and minds of participants.

Although many presentation trainers interpret delivery skills to be strictly verbal or physical, (voice inflection, hand movement, eye contact, gestures, etc.), I don't. I have witnessed hundreds of presentations, and I have seen very successful presentations delivered by people who did not have polished verbal or physical skills. I have observed presenters who were not overly articulate, somewhat shy, nervous, and even awkward—who were still successful. They were successful, despite their lack of verbal or physical presentation skills, because they had passion for their product or service. They were genuinely enthusiastic and positive about their topic and communicated their excitement to the audience.

According to studies conducted by UCLA professor Dr. Albert Mehrabian, only 7 percent of the feelings communicated in a spoken message are conveyed by words alone. Thirty-eight percent are communicated through the manner in which we speak, and the remaining 55 percent are conveyed nonverbally.

The fact is, nonverbal and nonphysical presentation skills are more important than verbal and physical presentation skills. This in no way diminishes the importance of having verbal and physical presentation skills, as I will address. It simply illustrates that the most important presentation skills are primarily nonverbal.

I attended a trade show and delivered a presentation about *The DNASelling Method* to a large group of bystanders. At the conclusion of the presentation, a neighboring booth attendee walked up to me and said, "I cannot get over how passionate you are about your program. You must really believe in it." I never forgot her statement. It makes my point—passion creates a sense of believability in the presenter and the product. When messages are delivered with passion, buyers feel that the presenter truly believes in the product or service being presented. Passionate presenters radiate genuine belief in the value of their product or service.

It would be difficult to exaggerate the importance of showing passion in sales presentations: *passion sells*. It creates a sense of believability and motivates people to take action. Look at Patrick Henry's "Liberty or Death" speech. It was the passion of his delivery that inspired the American Revolution.

Communicating passion is important because it prevents the cardinal sin of presenting—boring people. Buyers do not react well to presentations that sound dull, boring, or as if they are coming from an automated machine. Passionate presenters create energy, stimulate the thoughts and emotions of buyers, and engage participants.

Like passion, enthusiasm is communicated nonverbally. Enthusiasm is conveyed by a presenter's attitude and energy level. It creates an atmosphere of excitement, animation, and anticipation. Enthusiasm for the proposed solution is contagious. Typically, if the presenter is enthusiastic, the audience will be excited as well.

> **Caution!** Don't over do it. Enthusiasm is not being spastic, overbearing, or having "zeal without knowledge." Too much enthusiasm can actually detract from the impact of a message.

Be Positive and Optimistic

Although being positive and optimistic in a presentation seems fundamental, I mention it for one reason—most presenters do a poor job of developing and maintaining a positive presentation atmosphere.

Many sales presenters are far too serious, believing that they have to wear their "game face" to present. They are serious business people with facts and figures who are here to do their job! I have personally coached hundreds of salespeople in the art of persuasion. Consistently, I have had to recommend that they lighten up and not take themselves (or their audience) so seriously.

Mark Twain (Samuel Clemens) related an experience that makes my point: don't take matters too seriously in a presentation environment. In 1866, when Mark Twain was 31, he toured America, giving lectures about his travels throughout the world. The first speech he delivered was entitled "Our Fellow Savages in the Sandwich Islands," an account of his travels in Hawaii. As he concluded his remarks about some of the cultural and historical traits of the Pacific Islands, he said, "At this point in my lecture, in other cities, I usually illustrate cannibalism, but I am a stranger here and don't feel like taking liberties. Still, if anyone in the audience will lend me an infant, I will illustrate the matter."

Mark Twain knew that entertaining and educating are often one and the same.

> **Caution!** Taking matters too seriously can lead to dull presentations and bored listeners.

Of course, there is a time and place for seriousness in a sales presentation, but it is far more important to be positive and optimistic than to be serious. Being too serious can, in fact, hurt a presentation. Without sporadic injections of optimism and humor, a serious message can appear to be a negative message. Obviously, negative messages are not appealing to buyers, nor do buyers develop favorable impressions with negative presenters.

The key to projecting optimism is simple: smile. Be genuinely positive and upbeat. People react well to happy presenters, especially presenters with sincere smiles. It's almost as if they can't help themselves. A genuine, heart-felt smile is reassuring and fun. It makes a positive impact in the minds and hearts of participants.

The opposite is also true. Presenters lacking warm facial expressions, or failing to smile, project pessimism and negativity.

> **The Point?** Be positive and cheerful. Smile. Establish an upbeat, optimistic presentation atmosphere.

Communicate Confidence

In 1980, IBM was searching for an operating system to run its first personal computer. A group of IBM officials scheduled a trip to meet with the president of Digital Research, Gary Kildall. Digital Research was leading the personal computer software industry with its CP/M operating system. Fatefully, on the day of the scheduled meeting, Kildall decided to go fly his small hobby airplane rather than attend the presentation. Feeling snubbed, IBM decided to head north to meet with a small company in Seattle called Microsoft. During the Microsoft presentation, IBM announced its personal-computer designs to the president of Microsoft, Bill Gates. Gates boldly suggested that IBM rethink its strategy of using an 8-bit processor architecture. Instead, Gates recommended that they use the new 16-bit processor. Gates knew that if IBM chose to use the new 16-bit processor, they would also need a new operating system to run it. IBM took his advice, decided to use the 16-bit processor and awarded Gates the right to provide an operating system—an operating system Gates did not have! Regardless, Gates shook hands and agreed to deliver as promised. The rest is history.

The amazing part of Bill Gates' story is not his technology. It is his boldness and almost reckless self-confidence. IBM did not buy an operating system that day—they bought Bill Gates. They perceived the confidence he exuded when he gave his opinion and promised to deliver.

People like to buy from people who are confident because it's easy to believe confident people. Salespeople who deliver presentations with confidence communicate certainty and conviction. They convey competence and capability. People who ooze confidence communicate a strong belief in the value of their proposed product or service. The opposite is also true. Presenters who express self-doubt or communicate a lack of belief in themselves or their product create buyer uncertainty and doubt.

Don't confuse confidence with arrogance. Arrogant people are not likeable and do not communicate confidence. Instead, they generate resistance. No one wants to associate or do business with an arrogant, conceited, or egotistical salesperson. Genuinely confident people have a natural aura and attraction that is positive and appealing.

To communicate confidence, presenters must have confidence—real, genuine, self-confidence. There is no faking it. Buyers can sense false conviction. The only way to gain real, substantive confidence, is to be prepared, well versed in the topic at hand, and feel a genuine belief in the value of the proposed product or service. To develop confidence, presenters need to feel competent. You must study, practice, and rehearse your presentation prior to presenting.

Sales educator Earl Nightingale shared the following story, illustrating the power of confidence. There was a team of six American mountain climbers at the bottom of a mountain. A psychologist doing a survey asked each of them one question: "Can you make it to the top?" Five of the climbers answered with variations of, "I've been training for this for years. I'll make the best effort possible." One climber, however, answered simply, "Yes, I will." Not only was he the first climber to the mountaintop, he was the only one.

Over the years, I have come to appreciate the innate power of self-confidence. As a sales manager and executive, I have conducted hundreds of interviews. I have met and hired extraordinarily talented people. When I interview, I have learned to look for two primary characteristics: confidence and a sense of humor. I value those two attributes above all else—above experience, skills, even raw talent. I know that when I have a genuinely confident salesperson—coupled with a good sense of humor—I have the ingredients of a winner.

The Point? Confident presenters create confident buyers, communicate certainty, and develop a sense of believability in the value of the proposed product or service.

Use Appropriate Humor

Like passion and optimism, humor is an effective presentation and communication tool. Passionate, positive people are both likeable and believable. It is difficult not to like positive presenters. The same can be said of humorous presenters. It's difficult not to like a presenter who makes you feel good or laugh.

I cannot think of a single presentation skill that builds audience rapport faster than humor. Humor has an almost magical affect on people and develops a natural bond between presenters and participants.

Humor also provides participants with a mental recess during intense or detailed presentations. I have seen very tense presentations turn on a dime with a humorous statement.

> **Note:** Humor gains attention, creates rapport, and makes a presentation more memorable and entertaining. Used appropriately, humor can relieve tension, motivate buyers, and enhance the reputation of the presenter.

I have had training participants ask me, "If humor is so effective, why don't we see more entertaining and humorous presentations?" The reason is simple—with humor comes risk. Humor can backfire. Many presenters do not attempt to harness the power of humor because when humor fails, it can be awkward and embarrassing.

The key to using humor is to draw a clear distinction between appropriate and inappropriate humor. For example, some presenters use jokes. Jokes, however, are risky and should, in general, be avoided. Have you ever heard a presenter tell a joke that was not funny or relevant to the topic at hand? How did you feel? More than likely you felt embarrassed for the presenter. That's called bombing. Everyone knew the presenter was attempting to be funny, but no one laughed.

Most salespeople are not born comedians and run the risk of bombing with jokes. Even professional comedians who spend their lives perfecting the timing and delivery of jokes often fail. Celebrities like David Letterman and Jay Leno often deliver jokes that fall flat. Professional comedians can afford the occasional bomb. Sales presenters can't.

Of course, every presenter needs to avoid inappropriate humor. Inappropriate and offensive humor is dangerous and can taint a presenter. Humor that involves racial, religious, or gender related subject matter tends to lower the credibility of the presenter and turn off presentation participants. Humor should be used to build bridges, not burn them. Ethnic, racial, crass, or sexual humor should be completely avoided in sales presentations.

> **Note:** The primary rule for evaluating potentially offensive humor is, "When in doubt, leave it out."

The safest and most effective presentation humor involves entertaining stories and self-effacing humor. Poking a little fun at yourself is not only funny, it reflects self-confidence. This is one of the reasons people loved Ronald Reagan's humor. He poked fun at himself.

In addition to self-effacing humor, sharing entertaining stories can also be a fairly safe way to get an audience to laugh. I know a very successful salesperson who clips out humorous stories from *Reader's Digest* to use in presentations. Using *Reader's Digest* stories ensures that the stories are not offensive.

The point is to use appropriate humor to establish rapport and enhance the presentation experience.

Never Panic—Remember that Crisis Can Create Opportunity

When you struggle with a heckler, difficult questions, or a technical problem, never panic. Keep in mind that a crisis can create an opportunity.

Believe it or not, I actually welcome presentation problems. Seriously, I do. I have learned over the years that a problem or crisis can create an opportunity to show poise, demonstrate self-control, and use impromptu humor—all of which builds trust, increases credibility, and strengthens buyer-seller relationships. Presentation problems are opportunities because they take a presenter out of a controlled, artificial environment and place him or her on the spot. Suddenly, a presentation moves from being a rehearsed, scripted discussion to being an ad hoc situation. In other words, all pretenses are gone, and the audience is left to evaluate the "Real McCoy."

I learned a lesson about exploiting presentation problems on a business trip to Johannesburg, South Africa. I was delivering a presentation to over a hundred people in a major hotel when my power source died, and I was suddenly without a projector. Because our computer and AV equipment had traditional outlet extensions, our power source had to be converted from American outlets to South African. I wasn't sure I could fix the problem.

Rather than panicking, I smiled, told the audience to give me just a minute to address the situation, crawled under a table and began tinkering with our power exchange gadget. It worked! I stood up and proceeded with the presentation until it happened again. I told the audience that we would be taking a short recess and asked them to come back in five minutes. Once again, I fixed the power source. The audience came back, and I resumed my presentation. Of course, it happened a third time. This time I just stood there, shook my head a few times, looked up with a grin on my face and said, "Folks, have any of you ever conducted a presentation like this? Isn't this just the way it goes sometimes? Unbelievable." I once again crawled under the table and with a little duct tape (the greatest of all human inventions), fixed the problem.

At the conclusion of the presentation, I was expecting a "bomb." A 100% skunk! In spite of the problems, the opposite happened. It turned out to be one of the most successful sales presentations I have ever delivered. I was astonished.

On my eighteen-hour return flight to New York, I contemplated that presentation over and over. Why, with numerous delays and technical difficulties, was that, by far, the most successful presentation of my trip? Then, it dawned on me. It was because people had seen the real me. When the crisis hit, I was taken out of a comfortable, predictable environment and placed in a difficult situation. I was no longer a scripted, rehearsed, polished presenter. Instead, I was a regular person standing in front of them with a problem to solve. Because I did not panic, become flustered, or overly perturbed by the situation, I can only guess that they liked and respected my response. Maybe they even felt sympathy towards me. For whatever the reason, they bought, and they bought overwhelmingly.

Since that experience, I have noticed that every time I have a technical or related presentation difficulty, my sales actually increase. I have given it more thought since then and have developed a three-step guideline that I believe enhances the "crisis creates opportunity" theory. When you deal with a technical difficulty, stump the chump participant, or any other related problem, follow these simple guidelines:

1. Take ownership of the problem or situation. Don't ignore it. Don't pretend it doesn't exist. Be assertive in addressing the crisis and solving the problem.
2. Smile. Maintain your poise. Do not become verbally flustered, show facial expressions of anger, or become physically annoyed.
3. Have a sense of humor about it. Nothing diffuses an uncomfortable situation better than humor. Make light of the situation with a sarcastic statement, self-effacing joke, or simple laughter.

Distractions, problems, and difficult situations can be unnerving experiences for a presenter, but they can also be rewarding. Remember that a crisis can create an opportunity, garner sympathy votes, and when handled intelligently, increase the likelihood of delivering a successful presentation.

Voice Inflection, Eye Contact, and Body Language

I managed a very talented salesperson who was personable, hard working, and smart. In social settings, he was extremely outgoing. I attended a presentation with him on a major account and was shocked at his lackluster performance. He knew the product, the needs of his audience; he even knew the exact weaknesses of competing vendors. Unfortunately, even with all of his personality and knowledge, he was completely undermined by his delivery skills. He was boring! He was an entirely different person than the one I knew when he delivered his presentation. Rather than being vibrant, jovial, and confident, he was dull and uninteresting. He failed to vary the pitch of his voice and neglected to alter the speed of his speech. He didn't make eye contact with audience participants, and he even mumbled. At times, presentation participants had to strain just to hear him. It was terrible. We lost the sale.

Poor body language and monotone voices drain the life out of presentations, bore buyers, and completely alter the impact of a presentation message. How skillfully a presenter uses voice inflection and body language can be the difference between a stimulating presentation and a boring presentation—between winning and losing a sale.

> **Note:** Skilled presenters alter the pace of their speech, vary the pitch and volume of their voice, and strategically pause to accentuate major points of emphasis.

Presenters should speak loudly enough to be clearly heard and understood, and they should vary the pitch and intonation of their voice throughout the presentation. If a presenter's voice is high-pitched, nasal, strongly accented, or offensive, it will distract participants from focusing on the presentation.

Enunciation is also important. Slurred or mumbled words can irritate buyers and make presenters appear less credible and less authoritative. The opposite is also true. Exaggerated enunciation can make an audience feel like they are being patronized or denigrated. Skilled presenters avoid both extremes.

Speed and pace should also be considered. Presentations should maintain a comfortable verbal speed with alterations in the rate of delivery to add vocal and pace variety.

Eye contact is obviously fundamental to presenting. Presenters who fail to make eye contact with audience members do not project confidence. They may appear to have something to hide or look less than forthcoming. The key is to make eye contact with each member of an audience at least once for between three and five seconds and then briefly reestablish eye contact with participants throughout the presentation.

> **Caution!** Don't stare in any one direction or at any one participant for long periods of time.

In addition to voice inflection and eye contact, an added technique that communicates and builds rapport with buyers is to touch them. Of course I don't mean in a sensual or inappropriate way. I mean a simple touch on the arm or shoulder of a participant. A simple touch communicates a message of warmth and friendliness. Research by Dr. J. Hornik at the University of Chicago demonstrated that a light, brief (half second) touch on the upper arm of shoppers caused them to shop 63 percent longer and spend 23 percent more than people who had not been touched. A simple touch to an arm or shoulder is an appropriate and effective way to connect with an audience member

Use Effective Language

In the renaissance concept of education, knowledge and expression were much more closely identified with each other than they are now. To be educated was to be eloquent and to be eloquent conveyed a high degree of education.

No renaissance figure displayed better oratory skill or educational brilliance than Queen Elizabeth I. Queen Elizabeth's quick wit and flamboyant style have led contemporary annalists to treasure even her most casual statements. Elizabeth knew that leadership was largely a matter of communication, and that the more lucidly she communicated, the greater her ability to lead. Although few modern business schools teach eloquence, Queen Elizabeth was tutored by prominent classical scholars, most notably Roger Ascham, who held the office of public orator at Cambridge. Under his tutelage, Elizabeth became a renowned linguist and learned to communicate fluently in Latin, Greek, Spanish, and French. Her most acclaimed oratory fame, however, was her effective use of the English language. Queen Elizabeth crafted each formal utterance with careful precision and constructed complex and elaborate verbal edifices with unmatched competence. Her addresses to Parliament, dialogues with foreign dignitaries, and military speeches were filled with words, wit, and expressions that were inspiring, meaningful, and momentous. Queen Elizabeth's masterful use of language secured her reputation as the most eloquent monarch in British history.

Just as Queen Elizabeth I, modern presenters are judged by the words they use. Audience participants make personal and professional assessments based on a presenter's words, wit, and language. Presenters with a good vocabulary sound intelligent, informed, educated, and give themselves a competitive edge. Presenters with a poor or limited vocabulary sound unintelligent, uninformed, uneducated, and give competitors an edge.

The primary advantage of using language skillfully is better communication. Presenters with strong vocabularies not only sound more authoritative, they also communicate more expertly. Presenters who use a rich and diverse vocabulary are more descriptive and better able to verbally illustrate the benefits of proposed goods or services.

This is why I recommend memorizing and incorporating presentation *power words*. (See *Presentation Power Words* at the end of this chapter). Presentation power words enhance a presenter's ability to illustrate and describe proposed products or services. These words are verbs and adjectives that help presenters paint a vivid picture for buyers.

Purposefully using power words has an added benefit of streamlining a presenter's vocabulary and helping to eliminate any empty expressions, meaningless phrases, or unnecessary jargon that take up time without adding information to a message.

Using effective language does not mean using overly sophisticated or complicated language. Some presenters believe that using fancy words and elaborate terminology makes them expert communicators. Not true. A sure way to lose a sale is to make prospects feel stupid by using terms they may not understand. Using a varied vocabulary does not mean using overly complex, sophisticated, or technical terminology. Using a diverse vocabulary means using intelligent words that help communicate and clarify issues, not confuse or convolute them.

Choose Your Words Wisely

By July, 1945, the Japanese people were weary of war, and the Japanese government was ready to surrender. When Japanese leaders received unofficial word of the terms of surrender proposed by the Allied forces in Potsdam, they considered the terms fair and lenient. Japanese diplomats decided to withhold comment on the proposed terms, however, until they received an official ultimatum from the Allied High Command.

When he was questioned about the unofficial Potsdam Declaration, Japanese Premier Kantaro Suzuki attempted to maintain an air of neutrality. Unfortunately, in his response he used a word that has two meanings. He told a press conference that the Japanese government was adopting a position of *mokusatsu*. The word *mokusatsu* can mean to withhold comment for the moment, and it can also mean to ignore. The Japanese news agency mistakenly translated his comment to mean *ignore*. Radio Tokyo broadcast the translation to the world. Headlines around the world communicated that Japan was ignoring the declaration and rejecting the Potsdam surrender terms.

Based on the mistranslation, President Truman decided he had no choice but to use atomic weapons. More than a hundred thousand people were killed, and the cities of Hiroshima and Nagasaki were destroyed—in part because one diplomat chose the wrong word.

The words we use are directly correlated to the effectiveness of our communication. Presenters who use words that are precise, appropriate, and definitive have an advantage over competing presenters who don't. This is why skilled presenters purposefully place key words at select moments in a presentation—to enhance communication.

Words that do not improve communication or are subject to misinterpretation should be avoided. Theodore Roosevelt called such words *weasel words*. Roosevelt coined this term to describe "Words that destroy the force of a statement by equivocal qualification as a weasel ruins an egg by sucking out its content while leaving it superficially intact." Words such as "uh," "ah," "um," and "you know" are considered weasel words. They have no purpose and add no meaning to a conversation.

Be sure to avoid profanity. In any business scenario, especially in presentation situations, be certain to never curse or use slang. The use of profanity in a sales environment is offensive, unprofessional, and has no place in a sales presentation.

Caution! Avoid using words with which you are not familiar. Improper usage or mispronunciation of certain words can work against you. Rather then sounding intelligent, you will communicate that you are merely trying to sound intelligent.

In Summary

If two separate presenters deliver the exact presentation content, what makes one presentation better than the other? The answer is, of course, the delivery skills of the presenter.

Delivery skills add life and meaning to the content of a presentation. This is why all successful presenters share common delivery attributes. They show passion and enthusiasm for their product or service, are positive and optimistic, communicate confidence, utilize effective humor, and use appropriate variations of voice inflection, eye contact, and body language. In short, they implement winning delivery skills.

Presentation Power Words

Experienced
Authoritative
Accomplished
Celebrated
Renowned
Esteemed
Revered
Respected
Outstanding
Acclaimed
Prestigious
Recommended
Reputable
Competent
Dominant
Unprecedented
Exclusive
Uncomplicated
Clear
Simple
Effortless
Easy
Practical
Functional
Dependable
Usable
Applicable
Versatile
Strategic
Thorough
Luxurious
Splendid
Spectacular

Commanding
Phenomenal
Graceful
Sensational
Astonishing
Staggering
Dynamic
Sophisticated
Amazing
Fantastic
Awesome
Remarkable
Marvelous
Attractive
Appealing
Futuristic
Legendary
Authentic
Genuine
Honest
Valid
Legitimate
Proven
Tested
Superior
Reliable
Factual
Enormous
Complete
Striking
Encyclopedic
Unrivaled
Uncommon

Cerebral
Tremendous
Mammoth
Significant
Enriched
Enhanced
Superb
Finesse
Indispensable
Vital
Essential
Imperative
Invaluable
Crucial
Critical
Paramount
Exceptional
Unique
Excellent
Magnificent
Classic
Immaculate
Fabulous
Exciting
Extraordinary
Captivating
Exquisite
Distinguished
Stunning
Panoramic
Deluxe
Matchless
Compelling

Figure 11.1

Chapter 12

Features Versus Benefits

People don't buy Disneyland tickets, they buy fun.

—Anonymous

In 1487, Christopher Columbus managed to arrange a meeting with the monarchs of Spain—King Ferdinand and Queen Isabella. Columbus had spent years searching for financiers for his proposed voyage to discover a shorter route to Asia. He originally approached the Italian and Portuguese aristocracy for support, but to no avail. Eventually he finagled a meeting with the king of Portugal, John II. In his meeting with King John, he detailed his plans for the voyage and the necessary funding and equipment needed to accomplish his expedition. In return for financing the voyage, Columbus made serious demands on the king, including the title of Grand Admiral of the Oceanic Seas, the office of viceroy over the lands he discovered, and 10 percent of the future commerce with such lands.

After King John II declined his offer, Columbus decided to change his approach. Rather than talk about the details of the proposed voyage, he would focus exclusively on the financial benefits to the financiers, and the public glory associated with navigational discoveries. He decided to center his discussions on the interests of his audience—their greed, desire for fame, or need for wealth. His strategy worked magnificently.

Although Columbus was an unproven explorer, and knew less about oceanic navigation than the average sailor, in one area he was an absolute genius. Christopher Columbus knew how to persuade an audience. He had developed an amazing power to charm and convince his listeners by focusing on their vanity, conceit, and self-interest—and not his own. Queen Isabella was no exception. Columbus spent years in the queen's court convincing her of the financial and geopolitical benefits of establishing a shorter trade route to Asia. His strategy finally paid off. With the Spanish defeat of the Moorish invaders in 1492, and the wartime burden of the treasury lifted, King Ferdinand and Queen Isabella decided to patronize Columbus' maritime expedition. On August 3rd, 1492, Columbus set sail with three ships, equipment, the salary of the sailors, and a lucrative contract for himself. Although his mission failed to discover a shorter trade route to Asia, he made the most influential exploratory discovery of all time—the Americas.

Had Christopher Columbus continued making presentations focused on the details of the exploration instead of the financial benefits associated with funding the exploration, he probably would never have made his famous journey.

Columbus, however, was cerebral. He adjusted his approach and focused on the benefits the financiers would experience with the success of the proposed voyage rather than the features of the voyage itself.

Focus on Benefits

Every experienced sales presenter has been advised to "Focus on benefits, not features." Nevertheless, how many sales presenters actually know how to distinguish features from benefits? More importantly, how many of them implement the advice? Most salespeople repeatedly violate this principle, not because they disagree with the advice, but because they do not know *how* to implement it.

To avoid delivering a "feature bomb," sellers need to resist the natural instinct to jump in and tell buyers all about their good or service. For example, let's say a buyer shows an interest in a product by asking, "Does your air filtering system eliminate odors?" Non-cerebral salespeople immediately respond by providing a laundry list of capabilities. "Why of course. Our air filtering system not only eliminates odor, it also eradicates dust, fungus, and helps people with allergies breathe better. Not only that, this particular air filter..." Cerebral sellers, on the other hand, avoid delivering "data dumps" and instead question buyer inquiries. "Are you currently experiencing odor problems?" "How bad is it?" "What do you think might be the cause of the odor?" Rather than spewing a list of features, intelligent sellers identify the exact needs, concerns, and motives of buyers, and then address them.

A colleague asked me to assist him negotiate the purchase of a new truck. As he was examining a particular model, a salesperson approached him and said, "This truck has special equipment designed for pulling boats and trailers." My colleague responded, "I don't have a boat or a trailer, and I don't want to pay extra for features I won't use." By immediately hammering on the features of the truck, this salesperson actually deterred my colleague from buying.

I listened to a salesperson carry on and on about the capability of his customer service staff to support its clients in eleven languages. The buyer responded, "That's nice, but we only operate in the U.S. and don't need that."

There are multiple steps presenters should follow in order to drive home the benefits of their products and solutions rather than the features. The first step is identifying the needs, pains, and problems that buyers experience (see Chapter 4 on conducting an account needs-analysis). The second step is using the *Needs-Resolution Matrix* (see figure 12.1) to differentiate product features, advantages, and benefits—and then matching them to product solutions. The third step is using solution-benefit questions to help buyers see the benefits of implementing proposed solutions.

The Needs-Resolution Matrix

Rather than focusing on benefits and solutions, many presenters engage in low level feature wars that distract buyers from grasping the benefits of proposed solutions. More often than not, presenters just feature buyers to death.

> **Note:** People don't buy features. They buy benefits. They buy solutions to problems. The world's best product or service is worthless if it fails to solve a problem or satisfy a buyer's needs.

After a tour of duty overseas, a certain officer was appointed to a stateside induction center where he advised new recruits regarding their government benefits, specifically G.I. insurance. Within a few months, he had an almost one hundred percent sales record.

His supervisors were amazed at his extraordinary achievement. Rather than ask him how he accomplished such a remarkable rate of success, one of his superiors stood in the back of the room while the officer delivered his presentation. The officer introduced the general provisions of the G.I. insurance to the new recruit. He then concluded his presentation by saying, "If you buy G.I. insurance, go into battle and are killed, the government will have to pay $35,000 to your beneficiaries. If you don't buy G.I. insurance, go into battle and are killed, the government will only have to pay a maximum of $3,000. Now, which group of soldiers do you think will be sent into battle first?"

The key to focusing on benefits instead of features is to distinguish product benefits and features prior to presenting. The best way you can ensure that a presentation focuses on benefits is to clearly identify the benefits a product or service provides to a particular buyer before the presentation is delivered.

Differentiating benefits and features is not always as easy as it sounds. In order to assist presenters in making the distinction, I recommend using *The Needs-Resolution Matrix*. *The Needs-Resolution Matrix* is a sales, marketing and presentation tool designed to analyze products and services in problem-solving terms. It was created to assist sales and marketing professionals when they need to identify and understand the differences between buyer pains and problems, product features, advantages, and benefits.

The key to using *The Needs-Resolution Matrix* is focusing on client pains and problems first, addressing products, features, and advantages second. For example, list every possible problem and pain experienced by a client before analyzing the best product or features to address those pains and problems.

SONAR Opportunity Needs-Resolution Matrix[1]

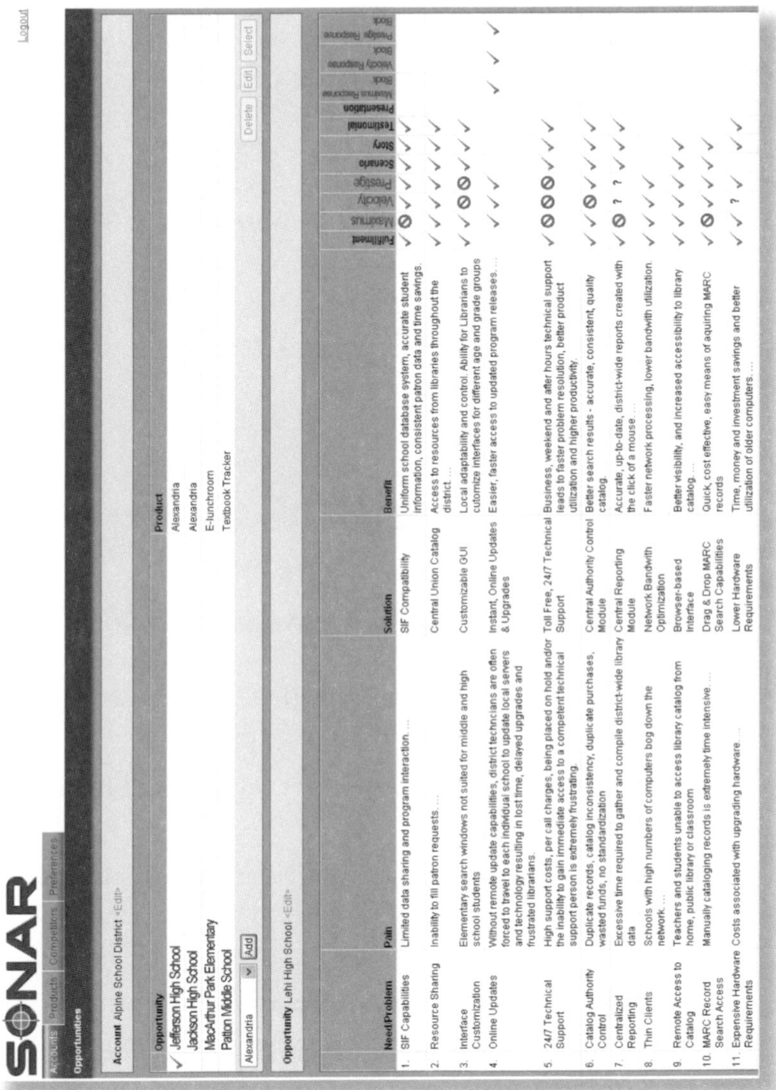

SONAR

Accounts | Products | Competitors | Preferences

Logout

Opportunities

Account Alpine School District <Edit>

	Opportunity	Product
✓	Jefferson High School	Alexandria
	Jackson High School	Alexandria
	MacArthur Park Elementary	E-lunchroom
	Patton Middle School	Textbook Tracker

Alexandria [Add] — Delete | Edit | Select

Opportunity Lehi High School <Edit>

	Need/Problem	Pain	Solution	Benefit	Fulfillment	Maximus	Velocity	Prestige	Scenario	Story	Testimonial	Presentation	Maximus Response Book	Velocity Response Book	Prestige Response Book
1.	SIF Capabilities	Limited data sharing and program interaction. …	SIF Compatibility	Uniform school database system, accurate student information, consistent patron data and time savings.	✓	⊘	✓	✓	✓	✓	✓				
2.	Resource Sharing	Inability to fill patron requests. …	Central Union Catalog	Access to resources from libraries throughout the district. …	✓	✓	✓	✓	✓	✓	✓				
3.	Interface Customization	Elementary search windows not suited for middle and high school students	Customizable GUI	Local adaptability and control. Ability for Librarians to cutomize interfaces for different age and grade groups	✓	✓	⊘	⊘	✓	✓	✓				
4.	Online Updates	Without remote update capabilities, district techncians are often forced to travel to each individual school to update local servers and technology resulting in lost time, delayed upgrades and frustrated librarians.	Instant, Online Updates & Upgrades	Easier, faster access to updated program releases. …		✓	✓	✓					✓	✓	✓
5.	24/7 Technical Support	High support costs, per call charges, being placed on hold and/or the inability to gain immediate access to a competent technical support person is extremely frustrating.	Toll Free, 24/7 Technical Support	Business, weekend and after hours technical support leads to faster problem resolution, better product utilization and higher productivity.	✓	⊘	⊘	⊘	✓	✓	✓				
6.	Catalog Authority Control	Duplicate records, catalog inconsistency, duplicate purchases, wasted funds, no standardization	Central Authority Control Module	Better search results - accurate, consistent, quality catalog.	✓	✓	⊘	✓	✓	✓	✓				
7.	Centralized Reporting	Excessive time required to gather and compile district-wide library data	Central Reporting Module	Accurate, up-to-date, district-wide reports created with the click of a mouse. …	✓	⊘	?	?	✓	✓	✓				
8.	Thin Clients	Schools with high numbers of computers bog down the network. …	Network Bandwith Optimization	Faster network processing, lower bandwith utilization.	✓	✓	✓	✓							
9.	Remote Access to Catalog	Teachers and students unable to access library catalog from home, public library or classroom	Browser-based Interface	Better visibility, and increased accessibility to library catalog. …	✓	✓	✓	✓	✓	✓					
10.	MARC Record Search Access	Manually cataloging records is extremely time intensive. …	Drag & Drop MARC Search Capabilities	Quick, cost effective, easy means of aquiring MARC records	✓	⊘	✓	✓	✓	✓					
11.	Expensive Hardware Requirements	Costs associated with upgrading hardware. …	Lower Hardware Requirements	Time, money and investment savings and better utilization of older computers. …	✓	✓	?	✓		✓	✓				

Figure 12.1

1. The *Needs-Resolution Matrix* is available electronically. For information visit, www.SonarSales.com or call 877-204-4341.

Category	Need-Problem	Pain	Solution	Benefit
The category of analysis: industry, market, business, department, end-user, etc.	A need, dissatisfaction, difficulty, or problem.	The result or consequence of unfulfilled needs &/or unresolved problems.	Product features & capabilities that address needs, problems, & pains.	The result of fulfilled needs, resolved problems & eliminated pain.
Department: Quality Control	*Updating Manufacturing safety documents*	*Failed FDA audit*	*Maximus Version 4.0*	*No more failed FDA audits due to poor safety document updates.*

Figure 12.2

There are five steps used in *The Needs-Resolution Matrix*:

1. Identify the *category* of analysis (business, department, person, job title, etc.).
2. Identify the *needs* and/or *problems* experienced by the category selection.
3. Identify the *pains* experienced by the category selection, i.e., the consequences of unfulfilled needs or unresolved problems.
4. Identify the *solution* that resolves the buyer's pain.
5. Identify the *benefits* to the buyer of fulfilling the need, resolving the problem, and eliminating the pain. hat resolve the buyer's pain.

Once you have identified client pains and problems, and the product features and advantages to resolve those pains and problems, you are prepared to create a winning presentation by incorporating the identified benefits into the presentation.

> **Note:** Benefits only apply to explicit needs. You may have some nifty features, but if product capabilities don't address specific client pains and problems, they are advantages, not benefits.

Information gathered from *The Needs-Resolution Matrix* equips presenters with the information needed to shift from the general to the specific. Presenters can take the general needs and pains of prospects and apply them to the specific capabilities and solutions of their products. Using this information, presenters can adapt the presentation to cover selected features that offer advantages relevant to the prospect's criteria, i.e., the benefits of the product or service. By keeping track of the needs and problems of buyers and then creating scripts and presentations to address and solve those needs and problems, sellers ensure that they focus their presentation efforts on the benefits of their solution.

Because product features are meaningless unless they help buyers eliminate pains and problems, winning presenters use *The Needs-Resolution Matrix* to demonstrate how their proposed products and features can fulfill needs, eliminate problems, and reduce pain—in other words, the benefits of the proposed product or service.

The FAR Strategy

After teaching salespeople how to use *The Needs-Resolution Matrix* to distinguish features, advantages, and benefits, savvy participants frequently ask, "What if you are uncertain about your prospect's awareness of potential advantages available with your product or service?" In other words, what if a product or service provides features and capabilities that could *potentially* solve problems that have not yet been identified? For example, software salespeople frequently run into this dilemma because software programs often have features and capabilities that provide solutions to problems that buyers weren't even aware existed.

When a presenter is uncertain about whether or not a feature is an advantage or benefit (remember that benefits are capabilities that solve *specific* problems expressed by buyers), I recommend using the FAR strategy. The FAR strategy is a simple, three step stratagem:

1. **Feature**—demonstrate the feature
2. **Advantage**—describe the advantage
3. **Response**—ask a thought provoking question to get the buyer's response

For example, if a presenter is uncertain of whether or not his audience needs a particular feature, he might say, "Let me take just a minute and demonstrate to you one of the capabilities X product provides that might be beneficial to your department. [Demonstrate the feature]. The advantage to using this feature is [describe the advantage]. What potential benefits do you see from implementing this capability? [Listen for the buyer's response]."

The pattern is simple: show the feature, discuss the capability, and emphasize the benefit. If the client responds positively, you have converted an unknown advantage into an explicit buyer benefit.

Solution-Benefit Questions

Review *The DNASelling Method*:

Discovery-Qualification Questions: Questions that discover a buyer's existing circumstance, account facts, qualification factors, and purchasing capabilities.

Need-Problem Questions: Questions that identify a buyer's needs, problems, and primary buying motives.

Ascertain-Pain Questions: Questions that ascertain the negative consequences of unfulfilled needs and/or unresolved problems, i.e., the pain.

Solution-Benefit Questions: Questions that focus on the benefits of need and problem resolution.

The final step of *The DNASelling Method* is asking solution-benefit questions. Solution-benefit questions focus on the value of solving problems and resolving pains. They center on the benefits of the presented solution. They move prospects from recognizing the impact of the current problems to focusing on the benefits of the recommended solution. *In other words, solution-benefit questions emphasize the positive benefits of solving identified problems.*

Sales professionals are often labeled and stereotyped as clones with habitual and predictable behavioral patterns. Unfortunately, the same can be said of buyers. Far too often, prospects focus on the minute details of product or service capabilities and fail to recognize or see the "big picture." It is a salesperson's job to move buyers away from understanding functional capabilities to understanding explicit product or service benefits. Sellers need to help prospects catch the vision of the product or service's benefits by asking solution-benefit questions.

The primary advantage of asking solution-benefit questions is getting prospects to verbalize product benefits. For instance, if a salesperson asks a buyer, "How would a faster network increase the productivity of your technical staff?" A buyer might respond, "It would definitely speed up the process of transferring large data files across our network." Solution-benefit questions get buyers to articulate the benefits of problem resolution and, in turn, convince themselves of the value of the solution.

Men are best convinced by reasons that they themselves discover.

—Benjamin Franklin

Although solution-benefit questions are primarily used during the investigation portion of the sales cycle, they can also be asked during the presenting and closing stage of the sales cycle. Many sellers ask solution-benefit questions during sales presentations to summarize topics, points, or benefits. They also ask the questions again at the conclusion of the presentation in order to sum up the benefits of the product or solution.

Sample *Solution-Benefit* Questions

After helping buyers ascertain the pain associated with the identified problem, cerebral sellers turn their attention to the benefits of implementing the solution by asking solution-benefit questions.[1]

What is it that you like most about our product?

What benefits do you see from resolving [X issue]?

How might this feature benefit you?

What problems do you see our solutions resolving?

How valuable would it be for you to be able to _____?

What other benefits do you see from using _____?

How will improving _____ affect your organization?

What do you see as the benefits of this approach?

What benefits do you see from implementing X capability?

How would _____ improve _____?

Is there any other way _____could help you?

Suppose you could eliminate _____, how beneficial would that be?

What is it about this solution that you find useful?

---

2. See Chapter 8 in *The DNASelling Method* to learn how to ask effective Ascertain-Pain and Solution-Benefit questions.

Suppose you could _____, how would that help you?

Is there any other way that _____ could help?

Because good questions don't just roll off the top of a presenter's head, it is important to develop solution-benefit questions prior to presenting. An excellent way to create solution-benefit questions is to identify ways in which your product or service benefits buyers. You can then convert those benefits into questions.

Note: Amateur salespeople sell products. Cerebral sales professionals sell solutions. Use the above questions to focus on benefits, solutions, and positive consequences associated with problem resolution.

Benefit Validation Statements

In addition to using solution-benefit questions, another useful, yet simple tactic for focusing on benefits and not features is using benefit validation statements. Benefit validation statements are short sentences that boldly state the benefits associated with product or service capabilities. Example benefit validation statements include:

The benefit of X capability to you is _____.

What this means to you is _____.

The benefit of implementing ABC product is _____.

Benefit validation statements help presenters communicate and emphasize the benefits linked to product features and capabilities. They are excellent tools for summarizing benefits.

Features: Don't Throw the Baby out with the Bath Water!

By emphasizing the importance of focusing on benefits, I am not implying that presenters should leave out any mention of the product features and capabilities that create the benefits. On the contrary, features form an important part of the presentation and the remainder of the sales process that follows. Features must be demonstrated, but only in order to focus on the benefits the buyer gains from using the product. Don't throw the baby out with the bathwater. Discuss and demonstrate features to introduce and validate the linked benefit.

As I previously addressed, features should rarely, if ever, be shown without an associated scenario. Scenarios help illustrate both the feature and the benefit as well as drive home the value of the proposed solution.

In Summary

For ultimate impact, presentations should address the needs, goals, and objectives of buyers and focus on the benefits buyers will experience by implementing your product or service.

Using *The Needs-Resolution Matrix*, presenters can clearly distinguish benefits from features. By asking solution-benefit questions, presenters help buyers articulate and verbalize product solutions. By selling solutions, presenters demonstrate the benefits associated with their product or service.

The Point? Remember: Disneyland doesn't sell rides—they sell fun. Black and Decker doesn't sell drills—they sell holes. Orthodontists don't sell braces—they sell smiles. People buy benefits, not features. Sell benefits.

Chapter 13

Slamming Competition with Grace

> *A great general establishes his position where he cannot be defeated. He misses no opportunity to exploit the weaknesses of his enemy. A winning general creates the conditions of victory before beginning the war. A losing general begins the war without knowing how to win it.*
>
> —Sun Tzu

In 60 B.C., Lucius Sergius Cataline attempted to exploit the economic unrest of Rome and incite an insurrection against the Roman republic. The ambitious politician conspired to burn Rome, overthrow the senate, and establish himself as the new protector of the Roman people. His was not an idle threat. Cataline had assembled a sizable army which laid in wait for an opportunity to strike.

Standing in his way was the elected consul of Rome, Marcus Tullius Cicero. Cicero was a well-known orator, statesman, and writer. He studied law, rhetoric, philosophy, and embarked upon a political career, attaining the consulship in 63 B.C. Cicero became aware of Cataline's plot through Fulvia, the mistress of one of the conspirators. After identifying Cataline as the primary conspirator, Cicero summoned the Senate to the temple of Jupiter in the capitol of Rome.

Realizing the volatility of the situation, and that many of the conspirators were in attendance, Cicero sought to inform the Senate of the seriousness of the conspiracy without simultaneously provoking the conspirators into action. With his usual eloquence, Cicero delivered the first of four indictments against Cataline and his plotters.

> I wish, O conscript fathers, to be merciful; I wish not to appear negligent amidst such danger to the State; but I do now accuse myself of remissness and culpable inactivity. A

camp is pitched in Italy, at the entrance of Etruria, in hostility to the republic; the number of the enemy increases every day; and yet, the general of that camp, the leader of those enemies, we see within the walls—ay, and even in the Senate—planning every day some internal injury to the republic… But if this man alone is removed from this piratical crew, we may appear, perhaps, for a short time relieved of fear and anxiety… I promise you this, that there shall be so much diligence in us the consuls, so much authority in you, so much virtue in the Roman knights, so much unanimity in all good men, that you shall see everything made plain and manifest by the departure of Cataline.

Cicero's address convinced an incredulous senate that the danger was real and that the planned coup d'état was already in action. Cataline was summarily sentenced to execution. He refused to surrender and died on the battlefield weeks later.

Embedded in Cicero's approach is an effective strategy to contend with competitors. Cicero used a *rational approach* to challenge and defeat his opponent.

Although dealing with competitors is not as dramatic as an attempted Roman coup d'état, most sales presenters regularly battle against aggressive, competent, and in some cases, unfortunately, unethical competitors. Knowing how to effectively neutralize and contend with those competitors is an invaluable sales and presentation skill.

Focusing on Competitive Differential Advantages

There is an age-old debate about directly mentioning competitors in sales presentations. Many presenters are fearful of bringing up competitors, and for good reason. If a presenter inappropriately or unprofessionally mentions a competitor, it can backfire and gain sympathy votes for opposing vendors. On the other hand, not making competitive comparisons is also a mistake.

The strategic objective of a sales presentation is to create a clear and unmistakable differential advantage between offered products and services and those belonging to competing products and services. Effective sales presenters focus on product benefits and emphasize capabilities that outperform competitors. Presenters must highlight their most compelling selling points and, simultaneously, expose their competitor's weakest points. These competitive differences are often referred to as CDA's (competitive differential advantages), POD's (points of difference), and USP's (unique selling points).

Note: Some basis of favorable differentiation is imperative to the success of a sales presentation.

Because most sales presentations involve competitors, presenters should focus on product or service benefits that are exclusive to the product or service they offer. Presenters should concentrate on their strongest competitive strengths and make clear and compelling differentiations between themselves and competing products and companies.

There are multiple manners of addressing competitors in a presentation setting. Some approaches are fairly low risk while others can be far more hazardous. There is one rule, however, that is universally accepted when dealing with competitors in a presentation environment: ***Negative statements about competitors generally hurt a presenter's credibility more than they hurt the competitor.*** Presenters need to be extremely cautious when directly mentioning or referencing competing products or vendors. When presenters discuss competitors too early, too often, or too aggressively, they may be perceived as being unprofessional or defensive.

Caution: Don't be baited into disparaging competitors. Any opportunity or request to attack competitors should be avoided. Instead, indirectly compliment competitors without diminishing your own product or service superiority.

In competitive sales, some basis of comparison is essential. It is important, therefore, for presenters to create appropriate game plans to handle comparisons in a professional, non-offensive manner.

There are three approaches to professionally address competitors in a sales presentation:

1. The soft approach
2. The rational approach
3. The triangulation approach

Each approach has its strengths and potential weaknesses. Depending on the style and personality of the presenter, and the temperament of the audience, certain approaches are more effective than others.

The Soft Approach

The soft approach attempts to emphasize competitive differential advantages *without mentioning competitors by name*. It is considered soft because it never directly identifies competing products, services, or vendors. Using the soft approach, presenters simply highlight products, features, and/or benefits that are unique to their offering—capabilities that are only available from the presented product or vendor.

The soft approach is a popular tactic because it is safe. It allows presenters to emphasize unique capabilities without potentially alienating an audience by directly referencing competitors. In other words, it's a low risk approach.

The downside to this strategy is the danger of not clearly and definitively identifying the distinguishing differences between competing products. If a presenter does not state the names of competing vendors or products, he or she must rely on an audience's ability to connect the dots and make its own comparisons.

> **Caution!** If a presenter is vague, ambiguous, or unclear when illustrating unique selling points, participants might simply assume that competitors offer the same capabilities or benefits.

The key to making the soft approach work is to define the language used to identify exclusive features and benefits—specifically the word *unique*. For example, in the introduction of a presentation, a presenter would say, "Today I am going to show you the benefits of implementing X product. I am going to demonstrate *unique* capabilities that are exclusive to, and only available from, Y Company. I'm going to illustrate why X product is the nation's leading widget, and I'm also going to use the word *unique* in a very strategic way. Every time I use the word *unique* to describe a feature, capability, or benefit, it means that the referenced feature, capability, or benefit is only available from us."

Presenters can then create, or ask participants to create, a visual "unique list." This list can be compiled on a flip chart, white board, even on a PowerPoint screen. Then, every time the word unique is used, the presenter purposefully pauses and says, "There is another benefit to add to your unique list." Or, "OK, here is another capability to add to your list of unique benefits."

The secret to using the soft approach is to ensure that the audience recognizes and understands the language used to highlight competitive differential advantages. Words such as *unique*, *only*, and *exclusive* should be used in sentences such as, "This capability is completely *unique* to X product." "We are the *only* supplier that provides this service." "This is a benefit provided *exclusively* by Y Company."

If the names of specific competitors are not going to be used or defined, then the language describing the unique selling points must be clearly emphasized.

The Rational Approach

The rational approach differs from the soft approach because it clearly identifies and directly mentions the names of competitors. However, it does so strategically and tactfully. Take, for example, Cicero's address to the Roman Senate. He used rationale to justify his position and then directly mentioned his opponent by name. The rational approach justifies mentioning the names of competitors by providing audience members with the reason and rationale for doing so.

The rational approach helps audience members understand that it is in their best interest for the presenter to make comparisons and differentiations between competing products. The advantage of this approach is that it allows a presenter to make clear product distinctions in a tactfully assertive manner. By providing presentation participants with rationale prior to directly mentioning competitors, presenters can soften the sometimes sensitive issue of directly addressing competitors.

Statements of rationale include:

> "I believe that I would be doing you and me a disservice if I did not point out the serious and significant differences between our product and X competitor."

> "Because we understand that you want to know the differences and not the similarities between competing products, I will be pointing out to you where X product is different and unique from Y competitor."

> "It doesn't make any sense for me to show how X product is like every other system. For both your benefit and mine, I will be demonstrating unique differences between X and Y products."

> "I wouldn't be doing my job if I didn't point out where X product is different and superior to Y competitor."

Caution! Be certain not to mention competitors that are not being evaluated.

By providing rationale, presenters "tee up" and soften statements used to distinguish their products from competing products.

Be sure that your comparisons are accurate when directly mentioning a competitor by name. I delivered a software presentation to a committee of technologists. Because I knew the competing vendors, I used the rational approach to lead into my comparisons. In one of my statements, I made a trivial (extremely trivial) mistake in my comparison. One of the committee members blurted out that I was misrepresenting my competitor. Although the erroneous statement was minor and insignificant, it killed my credibility, and I never recovered. The audience distrusted any further comparisons or capability claims I made.

The rational approach should only be used if the presenter is familiar with competing products. Without a clear understanding of competing goods and services, attempting to discuss competitors can be disastrous. Misstatements, erroneous comparisons, or false capability statements can lead to lost credibility, distrust, and buyer resentment.

The Triangulation Approach

One way to highlight product or service uniqueness—and to effectively emphasize competitive advantages—is to use the sales triangulation approach. This approach attempts to counter buyer efforts to "throw sellers into the herd" by distinguishing themselves from competitors and elevating themselves above competitors.

In the mid-nineties, the Clinton administration created a political tactic called triangulation. Triangulation elevated President Clinton above the political squabbling between Republicans and Democrats. Using the triangulation tactic, Clinton advisor Dick Morris and his acolytes portrayed President Clinton as a non-partisan, political expert above the fray of competing factions. Even though in reality President Clinton was a total partisan, he was depicted as an authority, a consultant, and a neutral arbiter.

His policies on welfare reform, homosexuals in the military, and other political "hot potatoes" were shaped by triangulation strategies.

In a similar manner, presentation triangulation positions the presenter at the top of the pyramid with competing vendors at the lower corners of the model. Triangulation positions presenters as consultative authority figures. By conveying an expertise of competing products and vendors, presenters establish themselves as industry experts rather than biased sellers.

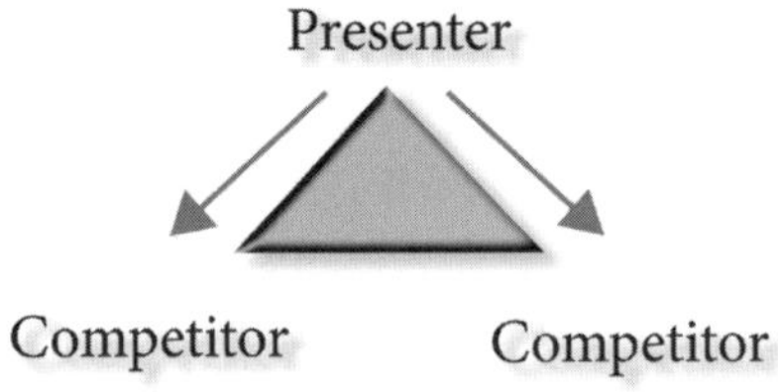

Figure 13.1

Presentation professionals who have a clear grasp of the capabilities and weaknesses of competing products or services can utilize the sales triangulation strategy.[1] Rather than engaging in petty feature wars, presenters can establish themselves as "non-partisan" authorities on the subject at hand. If you convey an expertise of both competitors and industry demands, you will establish yourself as a consultant rather than a biased seller. How do you accomplish this? By using strategic triangulation statements. For example, in reference to competing vendors, a presenter might say, "I am familiar with X and Y competitors. While they are both reputable companies, they fall short of addressing

1. Conducting a comprehensive competitive analysis and implementing effective competitive analysis strategies will be addressed in a forthcoming book, *MASS Marketing.*

ABC issue in the following way..." Or, "The norm in the industry is to address X problem in Y way. We, on the other hand, offer a completely unique approach that offers the following benefits..."

Triangulation places presenters above the fray and helps them separate from the pack.

Note: Sales triangulation should only be used by presenters who have a thorough knowledge of the weaknesses and vulnerabilities of competing products, services, and vendors.

Leaving Behind "The Bomb"

He will win who, prepared himself, waits to take the enemy unprepared.

—Sun Tzu

In the first month of 1864, an expert from the Confederate Torpedo Bureau entered the office of Jefferson Davis with a curious object: an iron casting, heavy and black that looked like a lump of coal. President Davis, turning the object in his hands, pronounced, "Perfection." It was a small bomb designed to be tossed into a Federal coal barge. When the object was shoveled into the enemy's warship boiler, it exploded with devastating power.

An extremely effective presentation strategy is to leave "the bomb," a strategically placed objection that a presenter leaves behind for his or her competitor. A presenter might, for instance, say to an audience, "When you evaluate competing products, be certain to ask about X capability." The suggestion allows a presenter to emphasize his or her own product strengths and bear down on a competitor's weaknesses.

Using this strategy, a presenter recommends questions and issues the buyer should ask all competitors—suggestions about requirements and capabilities that focus on the strengths of the presented product or service and the weaknesses of the competitors.

"The bomb" allows a seller to shape the battlefield without mentioning the name of a competitor. It is a preemptive strike that places land mines in the path of competing vendors. When a competitor arrives to deliver a presentation, he or she will be faced with a litany of questions and objections that highlight uncomfortable product limitations, inferior "work arounds," and/or product deficiencies.

In Summary

There is a fine line between being passive and proactive when dealing with competitors. Presenters who are too passive while addressing competitors fail to create clear product or service differential advantages. Presenters who are too aggressive when dealing with competitors come across as combative and negative and run the risk of potentially alienating potential buyers.

By using the soft, rational, or triangulation approach, presenters effectively address competitive weaknesses without offending or estranging audience participants. In short, they slam their competition with grace.

Chapter 14

Answering Difficult Questions & Overcoming "Stump the Chump" Tactics

In the middle of difficulty lies opportunity.

—Albert Einstein

Haile Selassie, ruler of Ethiopia for close to forty years, was once a young man named Lij Tafari. From an early age, Tafari exhibited a self-confidence and royal demeanor that surprised everyone around him. At the age of fourteen, he was invited to live in the royal court of King Menelik II. His intelligence, patience, and grace under fire impressed the King while inciting the jealousy of other young nobles. Envious of the attention King Menelik showered on Tafari, the young nobles physically threatened and verbally taunted the thin, bookish teenager. Tafari, though, never responded in anger. Instead, he showed an inward confidence and self-discipline that eventually gained the loyalty and allegiance of his peers. That loyalty propelled Lij Tafari into positions of enormous power. By 1930, he ruled all of Ethiopia.

In 1936, Fascist dictator Benito Mussolini invaded Ethiopia. Eager to demonstrate Italian ambition and to acquire foreign territory, the Italians quickly overran Ethiopian resistance. Lij Tafari was forced to flee.

While in exile, Tafari, who was now called Haile Selassie, addressed the League of Nations to plead his country's case. In a desperate attempt to gain international support and to condemn the unprovoked invasion by the Italians, Selassie made a passionate appeal to the members of the League of Nations.

The Italians, eager to suppress any negative publicity of the attack and to silence the unyielding Selassie, attempted to bully, intimidate, and prevent him from making the address. After numerous delays, the Italians finally allowed Selassie to speak. While speaking, however, Italian members of the

League of Nations heckled and insulted him with unrelenting abuse. Selassie refused to respond on their level. Instead, he maintained his poise and continued his address completely unaffected by their juvenile taunting. He went on to deliver a stirring speech on behalf of the people of Ethiopia and rallied public support in his favor.

Selassie's dignified pose and stately composure elevated his stature and credibility at the same time making his opponents look foolish and petty. Although powerless to take action (and based in large part to the dignity and demeanor of Selassie), the League of Nations recognized his appeal for support.

After World War II, and with international support, Haile Selassie once again ruled Ethiopia.

Behind Difficulty Lies Opportunity

Unfortunately, dealing with hostile audience members and fielding difficult questions is not reserved for political or public figures. It's a part of every presenter's job. Most presenters are faced with difficult questions and less than cooperative audience members on a fairly consistent basis. In spite of this, and as Haile Selassie demonstrated, *behind difficulty lies opportunity*. When presenters deal with difficult questions, unruly audience members, and awkward situations intelligently and professionally, they win over the hearts and minds of presentation participants.

Audience Participation

Determining the appropriate level of audience participation in a sales presentation is not without controversy. The debate about audience participation is as divisive as the dispute over directly mentioning competitors. Many presenters favor large doses of audience participation. Others loath participation—and for good reason. Too much participation can cause a presenter to lose control of an audience or topic.

Too little participation, on the other hand, can lead to boredom and a lackadaisical response on the part of participants. Finding the right balance is the key.

Although there are no hard and fast rules about audience participation, a generally accepted guideline is to have at least a modicum of audience involvement. As an old Chinese proverb says, "I hear and I forget, I see and I remember, I do and I understand." *Effective communication builds dialogue, not monologue.* People involved and included in a presentation are apt to build rapport with a speaker and connect with the product or service. In short, they are more likely to make a favorable purchasing decision.

> **Note:** Selling is not a spectator sport. Presentations that do not, in some way, involve audience members, are more prone to bore buyers and lead to unfavorable purchasing decisions.

Involving audience participants is not without risk. Presenters who do not control the amount of audience participation run the risk of losing control of the direction of the presentation. They might inadvertently provide participants with an opportunity to raise objections or encourage them to present difficult questions.

For that reason, presenters who choose to involve audience members need to control the participation, specifically the amount and type of participation. When a presenter senses that participation is getting out of hand, he or she needs to cut it off or limit the amount of involvement. When the level of audience participation begins to detract from the potential impact of the presentation, the presenter needs to regain control.

The most effective way to engage an audience is to simply ask easily answered questions. Easily answered questions prevent participants from providing long winded or drawn out answers. Presenters who ask easily answered questions encourage audience participation but limit and control the time involved in the participation.

> **Caution!** The bigger the audience, the bigger the risk of encouraging large doses of audience participation.

Presenters who are fearful of verbally losing control of an audience, but who still want to involve participants, can use non-verbal methods of participation. For example, a presenter can designate someone to keep track of time, have a participant run a keyboard or mouse, or assign someone to distribute handouts at the appropriate time. A presenter might hand out blank 3x5 cards prior to a presentation and have attendees fill out the cards with questions. This prevents attendees from shouting out questions in the middle of a presentation and allows a presenter to choose which questions to address.

The Proper Use of Handouts

Handouts play an important part in any sales presentation and, when used appropriately, are great tools for involving participants. The key to using handouts is focusing on how they are handed out. Far too many presenters simply distribute handouts before, during, or after a presentation, without giving due consideration to the impact the handouts will have on the audience.

The primary purpose for distributing handouts is to clarify and reinforce the focal points of a message. In a sales presentation, handouts help audience members understand and remember unique product or service benefits, core competencies, and competitive differential advantages.

The big question surrounding handouts is when to hand them out. This is a burning question because when handouts are distributed at the wrong time, they can be counter productive and distract buyers from the point of the presentation. If detailed handouts are provided at the beginning of a presentation, audience members will become over-involved in reading the materials instead of paying attention to the presenter. Handouts provided after a presentation, on the other hand, might simply be stuffed in a bag, or worse, in a garbage bin.

Encourage Participants to Take Notes

Research confirms that audience members who take notes become more involved and retain more information than participants who do not take notes. For this reason, sales presenters should provide an outline of the presentation with plenty of white space to take notes at the beginning of a presentation. Handouts should *outline* presentation topics and provide room for taking notes under each listed topic. In other words, the outline *should not* include every detail of the presentation. Instead, it should simply assist audience participants in following along, allowing them to take notes in the process.

If additional materials or details are needed to reinforce key points or ideas, subsequent handouts can be distributed when the important point or idea is presented. Providing subsequent handouts is particularly imperative when a presentation includes complicated, hard-to-understand, or very precise information that audience members will need to retain.

> **Note:** Providing outlines that encourage note taking is a smart way to improve retention, keep attendees involved, and help participants focus on key points of the presentation.

Many presenters use handouts to establish an educational tone to a presentation. The more that attendees feel a presentation is educational and not sales based, the less resistant they are to the presenter and the product. Appropriate handouts, workbooks, and other presentation related material reinforces the academic side of a presentation and lowers the resistance level of buyers.

Fielding Presentation Questions

Fielding questions during a presentation can be a sticky issue fraught with potential rewards and dangers. Although there are no hard and fast rules regarding how to field presentation questions, there are some general guidelines that should be followed.

Most importantly, a presenter must enhance the presentation, not detract from it, when he or she answers questions. For this reason, the decision to accept and answer questions during a presentation needs to be a predetermined, cerebral decision. Don't answer questions because you feel obligated to do so. If fielding questions will not help you achieve your presentation objectives, don't do it.

A significant determining factor when you decide whether or not to field questions is the size of the audience. Traditionally, the smaller the audience, the safer it is to address random questions. The opposite is also true. The larger the audience, the more dangerous answering random questions can be. If you are presenting to a committee of fewer than five people, for example, engaging in random questions during a presentation is not terribly risky. If, on the other hand, you are presenting to a committee with ten or fifteen members, fielding random questions might absorb inordinate amounts of time and detract from the overall impact of the presentation.

Some presenters find it useful to announce that they will take questions at the conclusion of their presentation during a question/answer period. Others find it helpful to announce that they will take questions at the end of each segment or session of a presentation. Announcing when questions will be answered allows a presenter to control both the allotted time for taking questions and the amount of time spent answering them.

I know a very successful presenter who insists it is better *not* to announce any "question rule" until questions become disruptive or distracting. Because he does not announce any rules in regard to answering questions, he provides an open forum that fosters natural audience involvement and participation. If the questions get out of hand or begin to detract from the presentation he simply announces, "Because most of the questions will be answered in the presentation, and because of time constraints, I would like to put off any remaining questions until the end of the presentation. Is that alright?"

The key to fielding questions is to determine your strategy before the presentation. Too many presenters get blind sided or thrown off track by audience questions because they fail to plan or prepare in advance to handle them.

Dealing with Difficult Questions

Fielding difficult presentation questions is like kicking field goals at the end of close football games or shooting free throws at the end of a basketball game with no time left on the clock. Depending on how the presenter responds, he or she will look like an experienced professional or an inexperienced amateur.

Dealing with difficult questions is challenging to all sales presenters, but the most difficult query to answer is the question you don't know the answer to. In sales presentations especially, it is important to not blow off or disregard questions simply because you do not know the answer. Evasive responses create evasive buyers.

When you must answer difficult questions, follow some simple guidelines:

1. *Restate the question*. Make sure you understand the question and that everyone in the audience heard the question correctly. By restating the question, presenters not only clarify the question, they also give themselves time to think about the answer.
2. *Don't guess.* If you don't know the answer, don't fake it. Offer to learn the answer and get it to the questioner. Write the question down and tell the questioner you'll have an answer for him or her in a specific period of time (24 hours always has a nice ring to it). By writing the question in plain view of the audience, you demonstrate to the questioner that the question was important and that you are serious about answering it. If audience members ask a question that you don't know how to answer, you might try to redirect the question by saying, "That's an interesting question. Does anyone have any thoughts on the subject?" Sometimes the audience can be a tremendous resource.
3. *Maintain your composure.* Do not verbally or physically flinch or become visually distressed or flustered. Maintain your poise.

4. *Always treat the question and the questioner with respect.*

While delivering a presentation to a group of entrepreneurs in Nashville, Tennessee, I had an audience member ask me a very difficult question. In a sense, he was challenging my expertise on the topic being discussed. Dead silence filled the room in anticipation of my answer. Rather than become defensive or belligerent toward the attendee, I simply responded, "I don't know the answer to your question, but I would be happy to spend a few minutes with you after the presentation to talk about it." I moved on. Had I become upset, embarrassed, or tried to fake an answer, the audience would have recognized it, and I would have lost credibility and possibly sales.

If the answer to a difficult question will detract from the impact of a presentation, offer to answer the question "off line." Tell the participant that you would be happy to spend a few minutes with him or her at the conclusion of the presentation.

Caution! Never attack the questioner. Even if a participant is a major jerk who asks difficult questions just to make you look bad, don't take the bait. The audience will recognize the person as a jerk. Keep your cool and don't become a jerk yourself.

Overcoming "Stump the Chumps"

Another difficult situation presenters face is dealing with "stump the chump" participants. A stump the chump attendee is typically a know-it-all who asks questions designed to make the presenter look like a chump. Stump the chumps use long-winded arguments, disingenuous statements, and manipulative tactics to discredit or embarrass presenters. Some of the more common stump the chump tricks of the trade include asking insincere questions, making snide or ridiculing remarks, or deliberately interrupting the speaker.

There are three general types of stump the chumps:

1. The Fool
2. The Joker
3. The Heckler

Overcoming the Fool

The fool is a presentation participant who unintentionally engages in disruptive behavior. The fool inadvertently asks unintelligent questions, makes irrelevant points, and/or utters distracting comments. Technically, the fool is not an official stump the chump because he or she does not purposely try to disrupt the presentation. Nevertheless, ignorance, lack of etiquette, or disregard for proper presentation proceedings can be devastating to a presenter who is unacquainted with appropriate responses or counter tactics.

I suggest responding to a fool's question or comment by reversing or redirecting the question or comment. For example, instead of answering a totally irrelevant question, a presenter might say, "The real question is…," or "The essential issue is…," or "Maybe what you meant to ask is…" If redirecting the question or comment doesn't work, you might suggest that the fool speak with you after the presentation. "If you want to discuss the issue with me afterwards, I'll be glad to talk to you then. Right now, though, I think that it's best for everyone involved to move on." The key to dealing with the fool is to maintain, and if necessary reclaim, control of the presentation by politely cutting him or her off.

> **Caution!** Remember your grade school teacher saying there's no such thing as a dumb question? She was wrong. There are plenty of dumb questions. Regardless of the idiocy of the query, always treat the questioner with dignity.

Be careful not become a fool yourself. I read about a public speaker whose response to a heckler perpetuated the heckling. When a participant interrupted a presentation he was delivering to a group of college students, he shouted, "Why is it that every time I open my mouth some jackass speaks!"

Overcoming the Joker

The second type of stump the chump is the joker. The joker is a class clown who wants attention. He or she uses sarcasm or tough questions designed to embarrass the presenter and display intelligence. Jokers attempt to "one-up" presenters and draw attention to themselves.

The most effective tactic to counter jokers is reverse ridicule. In other words, reverse the joke on the joker. Jokers hate to be laughed at. Presenters should do their best to respond with wit and acumen when dealing with jokers. You must place the burden back to them, and let them know that there are potential consequences (such as being embarrassed) for attempting to interrupt the presentation.

One of my favorite examples of a speaker using wit and acumen to silence a counterpart was delivered by Benjamin Disraeli. William Gladstone and Benjamin Disraeli were archrivals in the British Parliament. During one of their many debates, Gladstone yelled at Disraeli, "You, sir, will die either on the gallows or of some loathsome disease." To which Disraeli responded, "That, sir, depends upon whether I embrace your principles or your mistress."

Another famous retort was offered by Sir Winston Churchill in response to Lady Nancy Astor. At the conclusion of a heated debate between Lady Astor and Winston Churchill, Lady Astor stated, "If I were married to you, I'd put poison in your coffee." To which Churchill calmly replied, "Nancy, if you were my wife, I'd drink it."

For Civil War buffs, Alexander Hamilton Stephens provides a wonderful example of quick wit and a good rejoinder. Stephens stood only five feet tall and weighed less than one hundred pounds. He was, nevertheless, one of the intellectual giants of his generation. As a member of Congress from Georgia, he engaged in a series of public debates about The United States Constitution, state's rights, and the coming civil war. In 1859, while making a presentation to members of Congress, a political opponent and physically large man challenged Stephens. After insulting Stephen's small stature, the challenger threatened to, "Grease his ears and swallow him whole." Undeterred, Stephens replied, "You, sir, would then have more brains in your stomach than in your head."

Of course, not all presenters have the wit of Benjamin Disraeli, Winston Churchill, or Alexander Hamilton Stephens. That's OK. If a presenter is not capable or comfortable responding with sarcasm or counter rejoinders, he or she can appeal to the fairness and self-interest of an audience. For example, a presenter might respond to a joker by saying, "While I can appreciate your sense of humor, may I suggest that for the benefit of us all that we move on with the presentation uninterrupted by any further jokes or sarcasm?" The key is to get the audience behind you and help them see that it is in their best interest to move on with the presentation uninterrupted by the joker.

> **Caution!** Jokers are dangerous. They can taint your image and cause you to lose credibility. They need to be taken seriously and effectively neutralized immediately.

Like dealing with the fool, presenters might suggest that the joker speak with them after the presentation. "If you want to discuss this with me afterwards, I'll be glad to accommodate. However, right now I think it is in the best interest of all of us to move on." A presenter might also put the pressure back on the joker by asking, "What is your objective for being here today? Is it to learn more about X product? If so, may I suggest that we move on with the presentation?"

The key is to neutralize the joker as quickly and as effectively as possible. The joker must be neutralized as quickly as possible because if the he initially gets the response he is looking for, he will repeatedly attempt to draw attention to himself and away from the presenter or presentation.

Overcoming the Heckler

The heckler differs from both the fool and the joker in one primary way: for the heckler it's personal. For whatever reason, the heckler doesn't like the presenter, the presenter's product, the presenter's company, or the presenter's opinions. Because of the animosity he or she feels toward the presenter, the heckler is determined to humiliate or insult the presenter personally by disrupting or even preventing the presentation from happening. Hecklers come looking for a fight and will do anything to cause a commotion.

In 2000, I decided to run for office in my adopted state of Utah. As part of my campaign strategy, I held local cottage meetings to address the needs and issues important to my potential constituents. At one of my meetings, a man showed up who attempted to prevent me from conducting my meeting. He was apparently aware of my views from my political radio talk show program and came prepared to verbally do battle. A large audience was attending, and as I started my address, he began heckling me. He interrupted me and shouted his opposition to my candidacy. He did everything he could to prevent me from continuing. The crowd was clearly uncomfortable with the situation. After his first few outbursts, I looked at the audience and quoted a statement Thomas Jefferson once made, "Show me a man who has no enemies, and I will show you a man who stands for nothing." I then smiled and said, "Apparently, I already have a few enemies." The crowd applauded. After a few more interruptions, the crowd intervened and escorted the man from the premise. His antics actually won the crowd over for me.

The first rule for dealing with hecklers is to *stay calm*. Don't show anger. Remember the old maxim to "Smile at adversity." (If nothing else, smiling and staying calm will drive the heckler crazy). By not showing anger or responding rudely, presenters will not only counter the efforts of a heckler, they will also gain the respect of participants and get the audience in their corner. By remaining calm and in control, presenters can get audiences behind them and against the heckler.

The second rule for dealing with hecklers is to *not engage the heckler.* The response hecklers despise most is being ignored. If a presenter engages the heckler, he or she gives the heckler exactly what he wants. This is why every experienced presenter totally ignores the heckler individually. They do not ignore the heckling problem or situation, just the heckler. (If ignoring the heckler is not optional, e.g., the heckler physically or verbally blocks the presentation, cease presenting and seek an audience authority to deal with the heckler).

> **The Point?** Regardless of how belligerent a heckler becomes, do not become upset, flustered, or belligerent yourself. The more calm and cool you remain, the higher the likelihood of winning over the audience.

Agree with Thine Adversary Quickly

The Bible states, "Agree with thine adversary quickly, while thou art in the way with him…"[1] There are times when it is inappropriate and unwise to tangle with a vocal audience member. Take for example the experience of Frederick Douglas. While speaking at an abolitionist meeting in Boston in 1843, Douglas began making pessimistic comments regarding the possibility of ending slavery. Suddenly, an elderly black woman rose from her seat and hollered out, "Is God dead?" Frederick Douglas was an experienced speaker and had dealt with many awkward situations before. However, this woman's impassioned question momentarily stumped him. The audience then began applauding the woman and encouraging her to keep speaking.

1. Matthew 5:25

The woman who asked the question turned out to be no other than ardent abolitionist and former slave, Sojouner Truth.

If audience members verbally confront or challenge you, remember the advice of the Bible and agree with thine adversary quickly. Do not debate an audience member. If you do, you will force him to defend his position.

In Summary

Victory comes from finding opportunities in problems.

—Sun Tzu

The key to answering difficult questions and overcoming "stump the chump" tactics is being honest and smart. When participants ask difficult questions, don't try to fake an answer. If you don't know the answer, offer to get an answer in a specified time period. If that doesn't work, offer to answer the question "offline."

When dealing with hecklers, it may help to have a few stock phrases and responses in your arsenal to use when times get a little rough. Just be sure to stay calm. By maintaining your poise, you can turn a difficult situation into an opportunity to build credibility and win over the hearts and minds of audience participants.

Chapter 15

The Role of Credibility in a Sales Presentation

[The presenter's] character is the most potent of all the means of persuasion.

—Aristotle

In the early spring of 1783, in Newburgh, New York, a military coup nearly toppled the United States before it ever got started. In 1781, British general Charles Cornwallis surrendered to George Washington at Yorktown. As post war negotiations dragged on in Versailles, Washington kept most of his army intact. It was not, however, a tranquil time for Washington. The revolutionary war had wreaked havoc on the economy. While politicians bickered over the issue of forming a new government, the regulars remained poorly paid, and the officer corps were often not paid at all. Many of the regulars and officers had sacrificed much to serve their country. Homesteads were neglected, and in many cases, farms had been completely destroyed.

Having not been paid, a wave of discontent began to circulate throughout the army camps. Disgruntled officers flamed the passions of the restless soldiers. The officers saw the problem as purely political and reasoned that nothing would be solved under the existing loose confederation of states. They wanted a strong, central government that would clear the nation's debts, establish a unified economy, impose a reasonable tax system, and defend its hard-fought-for freedom from the territorial ambitions of Britain in the north, Spain in the south, and France in the west.

Plans were made to overthrow the existing confederacy and replace it with a temporary military regime. Letters circulated among the officers organizing the military takeover. The coup called for military forces to take the confederation's capital, Philadelphia, and on the same day take Boston, New York, and Richmond. A meeting was held on March 7, 1783, in Newburgh to solidify the details.

Although he was aware that his troops were disgruntled, Washington knew nothing of the planned insurrection until days before the coup when a trusted aide broke down and told Washington of the plot. Washington was appalled. He immediately summoned his officers and tried to dissuade them.

In his address, he assured his men that their complaints were just and that they would be heard "despite the slowness inherent in deliberative bodies." He urged his men not "to open the floodgates of civil disobedience, and deluge our rising empire in blood." Unfortunately, his words fell on deaf ears. At the end of his speech, Washington looked over the faces of his men and saw that he had failed to persuade them.

Desperate to stop the coup, he fumbled in his pocket to find a letter he had recently received from a congressman. As he opened the piece of paper and began reading, he realized it was not the congressman's letter. Washington appeared momentarily confused and perplexed. An awkward silence ensued. This shocked his troops. Through seven years of war, they had never seen their leader at a loss. Washington then reached into another pocket to retrieve his eyeglasses and, somewhat embarrassed, said to his men, "Permit me to put on my spectacles, for it seems I have not only grown gray, but almost blind in the service of my country."

As he looked up, he saw tears in the eyes of his men. Tears began to form in his own eyes, but he could not allow it. He gathered his belongings and briskly strode from the room. As he walked out, he was visibly moved by the scene of hardened soldiers with tears running down their cheeks.

Words were insufficient to stop the intended coup. It was the character and dignity of General Washington that proved too much for the conspiring officers. The coup was dead.

In the end, it was not an impassioned plea, a fancy quote, or an inspiring phrase that convinced Washington's men to retract their planned rebellion. It was the integrity, character, and credibility of Washington himself.

Character Matters

As Washington demonstrated, people are more influenced by character and credibility than by words or phrases.

People size up not only the content of what a person says, but also the character and trustworthiness of the person saying it. As Stephen R. Covey puts it in *The 7 Habits of Highly Effective People*, "It is character that communicates most eloquently… In the last analysis what we are communicates far more eloquently than anything we say or do. We all know it. There are people we trust absolutely because we know their character. Whether they're eloquent or not, whether they have the human relations techniques or not, we trust them, and we work successfully with them."[1]

It's really no different in sales. Buyers form immediate impressions about presenters. They determine whether or not the presenter sounds intelligent or ignorant, friendly or conceited. Buyers even form opinions about presenters based on appearance and dress. No impression, however, is more critical to the success of the presenter than credibility.

> **Note:** Credibility is the impression people form about you, your company, and your product. It's a sense of believability, trustworthiness, and perceived competence. It resonates from your countenance, voice, language, and demeanor.

1. Stephen R. Covey, *The 7 Habits of Highly Effective People* (New York: Simon and Schuster, 1989) 22.

There are two reasons credibility is important to successful sales presentations:

1. *Credibility helps establish presenters as consultants rather than biased product "pushers" or manipulative sellers.* Credibility is a prerequisite to any buyer-seller relationship and forms the foundation of long-term relationships. The key to building effective relationships in any sales situation is establishing credibility early in the selling process.
2. *Credibility sells.* The greater the credibility of the presenter, the more value prospects attach to the information presented. Without credibility, buyers won't trust the motives, intentions, or recommendations of presenters. In any sales situation, credibility must be firmly established for the sale to advance. Presenters who don't create credibility won't make it to the closing stage of the sales cycle.

Unfortunately, establishing credibility sounds easier than it really is. Buyers are automatically suspect of the intentions of sales presenters. If a buyer feels a presenter has anything less than forthright motives for making the product recommendation, the credibility of the presenter is diminished and so is the likelihood of making the sale.

Note: Presenters are subject to Napoleonic Law—guilty until proven innocent. Most buyers are automatically suspect of salespeople. Sales professionals must overcome this stigma by establishing credibility early in the presentation.

There are three primary components of sales related credibility:

1. Character
2. Product knowledge
3. The proper use of testimonials

Character

What you are shouts so loudly in my ears I cannot hear what you say.

—Emerson

It is character and honesty that give life to professional presentation skills. Without sincerity and character, potential clients interpret presentation techniques as manipulative and duplicitous.

The number one key to success in sales is motivating people to like you and to trust you. You have undoubtedly heard the oft-repeated selling adage, "People buy from people they trust." A person with character is a person who can be trusted. Far too often this simple reality is overlooked.

In the first few minutes of a presentation, buyers make assessments about presenters. The most important assessment buyers make regards the character of the presenter. Presentation participants need to feel that presenters are honest and trustworthy. If presenters use manipulative tactics or pushy techniques, buyers won't trust them. If presenters sound like "oily opportunists," or if they are phony or insincere, buyers won't trust them. If presenters do anything that indicates a lack of character or integrity—such as lying, misleading, exaggerating, acting phony or artificial—buyers won't trust their motives or recommendations. Without trust in the presenter's character, there will be little-to-no confidence in the value of the proposed solutions or disseminated information.

> **Note:** In the initial stages of the presentation, too many sellers focus on selling their products instead of selling themselves.

Product Knowledge

Product knowledge is the second component of sales related credibility. In order to establish credibility, presenters need to demonstrate in-depth product knowledge and utilize correct terminology as it relates to the buyer's business or situation. When presenters fail to display adequate product or market knowledge, buyers feel uncomfortable accepting recommended proposals or solutions.

What if I told you I was a big fan of tennis? You have no reason to doubt it. For all you know, I was once a professional tennis player. You would probably believe me, right? What if we were conversing about tennis and I said to you, "Wasn't that great when Andre Agassi came back after being down four to nothing?" Now do you believe that I'm a huge fan of tennis?

For those of you familiar with how tennis is scored, you already know that I do not know what I'm talking about.

Presenters not only communicate their level of product related knowledge with language, they also communicate expertise with presentation content. Words, questions, and comments reflect the level of experience a person has in any particular industry. Familiarizing yourself with appropriate market terminology is mandatory. By studying product literature and memorizing key words, concepts, and market specific phrases, presenters enhance their ability to establish credibility early in the presentation.

> **Note:** Demonstrating industry-specific knowledge is crucial to establishing credibility. Understanding buyer needs and using industry specific-terminology indicates expertise that will be of value to the buyer.

In the presentation stage of the sales cycle, the person doing the presenting must be knowledgeable concerning the product, market, and needs of the presentation participants. The presenter must be able to answer questions, address objections, and provide detailed information about the proposed product or service. Presenters should be able to answer both simple and in-depth questions pertaining to product and service capabilities. Superficial product or service knowledge undermines the credibility of both message and messenger.

Testimonials

As I discussed in Chapter 9, testimonials are wonderful sales tools. A quote or statement by a reputable customer can establish the value and credibility of a presented good or service far more effectively than the lone words of a presenter. Consider the saying, "A whisper by a satisfied customer is louder than a shout by a self interested salesperson."

It is not only important to establish personal credibility in a presentation, but it's equally important to establish corporate credibility. To establish corporate credibility, display a testimonial letter from an ecstatic customer or a list of existing clients for buyers to reference. Testimonials can be displayed on a PowerPoint screen, on an overhead projector, or distributed via a handout.

Testimonials are extremely powerful tools. A testimonial from a senior level person on the letterhead of a well-known company gives presenters and businesses credibility. Used appropriately, client testimonials substantiate and support the claims of the presenter and establish personal, product, and corporate credibility. Testimonials provide supporting evidence to validate the benefits associated with the presented product or service. Presenters communicate benefits available to the audience by illustrating how the proposed product or business has similarly benefited other people or organizations. Testimonials build credibility and validate product or service claims in addition to building trust between buyers and presenters. Be sure to incorporate testimonials into your presentation.

In Summary

People are more influenced by the character and credibility of a presenter than by the words or phrases he or she uses. Credibility is the impression people form about the presenter and the proposed product or service. It establishes a sense of believability and resonates from the presenter's voice and demeanor. It has a tremendous influence over the outcome of a presentation, and ultimately, a sale.

The Point? As credibility is built, so is the value a prospect associates with the proposed solution. Establish credibility by projecting character, demonstrating industry and product related knowledge, and using client testimonials.

Follow-Up & Implementation

16. Presentation Evaluations & Follow-up
17. The Ten Commandments of Presenting
18. Implementing Winning Presentation Skills

Chapter 16

Presentation Evaluations & Follow-up

Honest criticism is hard to take, particularly from a relative, a friend, an acquaintance, or a stranger.

—Franklin P. Jones

In 1814, Coalition forces from Prussia, Russia, Britain, and Sweden invaded France and marched on Paris. After twenty-one years of warfare, Napoleon Bonaparte was finally forced to abdicate and was exiled to the British controlled island of Elba. Astoundingly, in 1815, he was rescued from the island, resumed control of France and attacked the Coalition army in Belgium. On June 18th, the battle of Waterloo ensued when British commander Arthur Wellington counter attacked Napoleon. The fate of nations hung in the balance. If victorious, Napoleon would bring another decade of war and conquest. If defeated, Europe could once again experience peace.

Perhaps no one had more riding on the battle than Nathan Rothschild. The London branch of the great Rothschild banking house had taken a keen interest in Wellington's attack. Nathan Rothschild had staked the family fortune on arming and supplying Wellington's vast army and had done so with British bonds. Because the house of Rothschild was the largest single holder of British bonds, the outcome of the battle of Waterloo would forever alter their financial fate.

Nathan Rothschild was no fool. He and his family had developed a vast network of European informants and had created their own private messenger service. Day and night, the blue uniforms of the Rothschild couriers could be seen in coaches and in ships carrying messages, information, securities, notes, debts, and orders to buy or sell. Of all the information his agents delivered, however, none was more important than the news they carried about battles, warfare, and weather—news that moved markets.

On the morning following Wellington's attack, the 19th of June, 1815, Nathan Rothschild slipped out of London and made his way to the Folkestone harbor in order to receive news from the other side of the English Channel. A few hours later, a Rothschild's agent arrived and handed him a Dutch gazette newspaper with news of the battle. After scanning the headlines, he sped back to the London Exchange.

As he entered the Exchange, anticipation filled the room. The Rothschild reputation for inside information was well established, and investors knew the stakes that day were high. Rothschild maintained a calm but stoic expression and then motioned to his brokers to begin selling his British bonds. This could only mean one thing: Wellington had been defeated. Panic struck the Exchange as Rothschild continued to sell, and sell, and sell more. Bond prices collapsed.

With the price of bonds almost completely worthless, Rothschild suddenly reversed course and bought every British bond on the market—hundreds of thousands of pounds worth of bonds. Moments later, and after Rothschild had cornered the entire British bond market, news of Napoleon's defeat surfaced.

Because of the information network the Rothschild's had developed, on one day, and with one bold stroke, the Rothschild family treasury was transformed into one of the world's largest fortunes in history.

The Power of Information and Accurate Feedback

The point of the story of Nathan Rothschild and the battle of Waterloo is this: accurate feedback can pay big dividends. People and organizations constantly searching for feedback and information to improve their performance and existing situation have a competitive edge over those people and organizations that don't. Successful presenters should always encourage audience feedback in order to improve performance. Presenters need honest criticism to learn, grow, and educate themselves on their presentation strengths and weaknesses. Without accurate feedback, a presenter will not have the data to make necessary improvements or changes.

Delivering presentations without obtaining audience feedback is like running without keeping time. It's like playing baseball without calculating batting averages or playing golf without a scorecard. Evaluations are nothing more than a presenter's ability to keep score.

There are two types of presentation evaluations. The first is a presenter's self-evaluation. If you are like most presenters, the end of a presentation signals the start of your brilliant hindsight. After each presentation, winning presenters go through the mental process of critiquing their own presentation. They ask self-evaluation questions such as, "Did my presentation establish and retain the audience's attention?" "Did my presentation offer solutions that related directly to the needs, pains, and problems of the buyers?" "Did my presentation create competitive differential advantages and give the audience a compelling reason to purchase my good or service?"

The second evaluation should come from audience participants. Most successful presenters take the time to self evaluate their performance but make the mistake of failing to solicit the feedback of audience members.

Evaluation forms that provide attendees with an opportunity to provide comments, suggestions, and feedback to the presenter should be handed out at the conclusion of each presentation.

I regularly hand out evaluation forms following my presentations. Years ago I received an evaluation form back that shocked me. The participant who filled out the form kept track of the number of times I used, what (to my embarrassment), was a terrible phrase. I had used a distasteful phrase to illustrate the rigidity of my competitor's program. I was not even aware that I was using the term. Had the attendee not provided me with that feedback, I probably would have blindly continued to use a distasteful term that was offensive to audience members.

Evaluation Forms

There are a few guidelines presenters should follow when providing evaluation forms (sometimes called feedback forms). First, keep the evaluation form simple. Evaluation forms should be uncomplicated, short, and to the point. Typically, they should contain no more than six or seven questions. If evaluation forms are lengthy, overly detailed or confusing, presentation participants will not take the time to make honest observations or provide substantive feedback.

Second, keep the evaluation form anonymous. Many buyers will not provide honest feedback if they have to put their name on the evaluation form.

Third, make sure that the evaluation form can be mailed to the presenter at the participant's convenience. Many buyers will not want to be rushed during the evaluation. They might have seen something in the presentation that really bothered them or that really excited them, and this is their opportunity to express their opinion. Create a form that can be mailed or handed in at their convenience.

> **Note:** Evaluation forms can also be used to obtain leads and referrals. There is no better time to ask for referrals than at the conclusion of a well-executed presentation.

Post-presentation Follow-up

Building relationships is at the heart of successful selling. This is why, after a presentation, it is important to continue building relationships by continuing the communication process. Send post-presentation thank-you notes, letters, and/or emails to develop and strengthen relationships. When sales professionals engage in post presentation activities, they gain "mind share," and help buyers understand the presenters' level of commitment to the account.

Persistence and professionalism are crucial to post-presentation follow-ups Presenters should, without exception, follow-up presentations with letters, emails, literature, and messages that are specific to the needs of the different presentation attendees. Whenever possible, presenters should customize follow-up correspondence to each participant.

Sample Presentation Evaluation Form

Presenter

Did the presenter make a good first impression?

Poor 1 2 3 4 5 6 7 8 9 Great

Was the presenter knowledgeable?

Poor 1 2 3 4 5 6 7 8 9 Great

Was the presenter effective?

Poor 1 2 3 4 5 6 7 8 9 Great

Content

Were your needs and interests adequately addressed?

Poor 1 2 3 4 5 6 7 8 9 Great

How would you rate the overall presentation?

Poor 1 2 3 4 5 6 7 8 9 Great

What did you enjoy most about the presentation?

Are there any comments or recommendations you would offer the presenter to help improve the presentation?

Thank you for your feedback. It is greatly appreciated.

Patrick Henry Hansen

After a presentation, a presenter might make notes regarding questions or comments made by specific audience members. He or she can then write a personal thank-you note or send an email that mentions the question or comment.

Thank-you Notes

When it comes to follow-up, the little things develop into the big things. The more personal and detailed a presenter can make post presentation correspondence, the better. This is why, in addition to sending a formal follow-up letter, I recommend sending personalized thank-you notes as well. Thank-you notes add a personal and emotional touch that buyers appreciate. Buyers know that the presenter cared enough to take the time to send a friendly message of appreciation.

Warm and fuzzy thank-you notes should be a permanent part of every presenter's repertoire. The modest thank-you note is deceptively effective for building personal and professional relationships. When someone takes the time to send you a genuine thank-you note, how do you feel? Like all human beings, you feel warm and appreciative. Does that mean buyers will be more receptive to your calls and questions? Probably. The point is, you can't go wrong by thanking someone for a presentation opportunity. It adds a touch of professionalism and class. It makes the sale more personal and builds relationships. You also have the opportunity to outshine competitors by going the extra mile.

> **The Point?** A timely thank-you note or thoughtful telephone call not only demonstrates proper business etiquette, it also provides an opportunity for sellers to outperform competitors.

In Summary

Winning presenters are persistently looking for ways to improve, and what better way to improve than by gaining feedback from the very people presenters are attempting to persuade? Evaluation forms are like presentation mirrors that reflect back the good, the bad, and the ugly—information you need to improve your presentation skills, delivery, and content.

Following up is also an essential step to being a professional presenter. Be sure to send simple thank-you notes, emails, and formal follow-up letters to strengthen relationships and advance sales from the presentation stage of the sales cycle to the closing stage of the sales cycle.

Sample Post-Presentation Follow-up Letter

April 9, 2006

Mike Ricks
Director of Sales
World Alliance
25 North State Street
St. Louis, MO. 63179

Dear Mike,

It was a pleasure meeting with you and the training committee yesterday. I'm pleased that we had an opportunity to discuss some of the ways in which *Patrick Henry & Associates* can be of service to World Alliance. I am confident our advanced sales and negotiation trainings will improve your bottom line.

Enclosed is the proposal I promised to send, outlining the costs associated with the various trainings we discussed. Also included is the projected increase in sales and a return on investment sheet.

For more information, please contact me via telephone or visit our Web site, www.PatrickHenryInc.com.

Again, thank you for the opportunity to present our corporate training program to your committee. I look forward to working with you.

Best regards,

Derris Moore

Derris Moore
Account Executive
Patrick Henry & Associates, Inc.
Phone: 1 (877) 204-4341
dmoore@PatrickHenryInc.com

Chapter 17

The Ten Commandments of Presenting

Forewarned is forearmed.

—Anonymous

As a child in Egypt, Moses was saved from the slaughter of all male Israelite children by being hidden in the bulrushes along the Nile. He was found by one of Pharaoh's daughters and raised in the Egyptian court. He later became the prophet and lawgiver of the Israelites and led them out of Egypt. After wandering in the wilderness for forty years, the Israelites approached the promised land of Canaan.

In an attempt to communicate with God, Moses climbed Mount Sinai. There, Jehovah gave him Ten Commandments for the Israelites to keep in order to maintain their favorability with God. Throughout their history, when the Israelites obeyed the Ten Commandments, they flourished. When they disobeyed the Ten Commandments, they floundered.

Similarly, *The Ten Commandments of Presenting* are proven formulas and tested presentation principles that lead to success. By following *The Ten Commandments of Presenting,* winning presenters achieve predictable presentation results. By violating *The Ten Commandments of Presenting*, presenters proceed at their own risk.

Commandment 1: Be Prepared

Every battle is won before it's ever fought.

—Sun Tzu

As a young man, Demosthenes (383-322 B.C.) attempted to persuade Athenian leaders to resist the military ambitions of Phillip of Macedon (father of Alexander the Great). As he addressed the Athenian assembly, his voice was weak, his manner timid, his thoughts muddled, and he spoke with a stammer. When he finished his speech, the crowed booed him off the platform.

As he was ushered off the stage, he promised himself: "Never again will I speak unprepared!" And prepare he did. He cultivated his voice by shouting at the top of his lungs into the Aegean Sea. He practiced his speeches under a dangling sword to bolster his courage. He trained with pebbles in his mouth to eliminate his speech impediment. Years later, he fully vindicated himself by delivering an oratorical masterpiece entitled, *On the Crown*. With eloquent words, powerful voice, and stately manner, he drew uproarious cheers from the audience and went on to become the greatest orator of Classical Greece.

In just about any endeavor, *preparation precedes power*. In presentations, though, preparation plays an especially important role. It takes time and preparation to create an effective presentation outline. It takes time and preparation to develop a powerful introduction, content-rich message, and memorable conclusion. It takes time and preparation to rehearse and master the delivery of a presentation.

Confidence flows from preparation. The only way to present with confidence is to feel confident. There is no shortcut. To feel confident, presenters need to feel mentally prepared and well versed in the topic, subject, or product being presented. Ample preparation is often the competitive edge that tips buyers in favor of purchasing your good or service.

The Point? Successful presenters are prepared presenters.

Commandment 2: Rehearse, Rehearse, Rehearse

All the world's a stage, and most of us need more rehearsals.

—Anonymous

The skills that raise a presentation from mediocre to memorable are spontaneity, audience interaction, and *mastering* the material, not just memorizing it. Rehearsing is fundamentally important in order to attain mastery. The presentation will be natural and spontaneous only if you invest time rehearsing, memorizing content, and timing the delivery of the message. Ironically, the more time presenters spend rehearsing presentations, the less rehearsed they sound. Because they have mastered the content and memorized the chronology of the presentation, they are more spontaneous and natural.

Keep in mind that the primary purpose for rehearsing is to memorize the order and structure of the presentation content. This allows a presenter to fine tune the content of the presentation and ensures that the major points of emphasis are delivered at the right time and with the weight and significance intended.

When possible, presenters should rehearse their presentation in front of an audience. An audience (especially an audience of peers) will supply presenters with honest and constructive criticism and point out areas that need improvement. An audience will also provide feedback about any annoying or distracting verbal or physical mannerisms.

If an audience of peers isn't feasible, presenters should audio or video tape a rehearsal. Audio and videotapes help presenters identify delivery mistakes and correct them prior to presenting. Based on their own critique, presenters can correct any undesirable verbal or physical delivery behaviors.

The Point? Don't leave presentation success to chance. Practice and rehearse your presentation to master content and refine delivery skills.

Commandment 3: Create a Presentation Outline

The Marriott Courtyard Hotel chain used to run television advertisements that illustrated a fear every presenter experiences. The commercial showed a business executive delivering a presentation. He began by saying, "There are three points I want to emphasize today." After stating the first point, he would forget the second and third points. While standing at the podium with an awkward, uncomfortable look on his face, a voice-over would comment, "Never underestimate a good night's rest."

Regardless of how much a presenter rehearses a presentation, there is still room for error and forgetfulness. For this reason, winning presenters use outlines. They know it is only a matter of time before they experience a "brain cramp," forget their next point, or lose their place in the presentation. (Outlines are especially important for presentations to large audiences and/or committees).

An outline is like a blueprint for a home. It provides the framework and basic structure of a presentation. It helps organize thoughts, themes, and topic chronology. Outlines are used not only to create a presentation framework, but also as a reference tool to be used *during* a presentation. When a presenter has a mental lapse or gets mentally flustered, he or she can quickly reference the outline, regain composure, and move on with the presentation. Outlines also ensure that presenters do not forget to present or highlight major points or topics of discussion.

Cerebral sellers understand that there are no second chances when it comes to presenting. You only get one shot to advance a sale. Outlines ensure that you make the most of the opportunity.

The Point? Create an outline to highlight unique product capabilities, emphasize competitive advantages, and to fall back on in case of forgetfulness.

Commandment 4: Avoid Generic Presentations—Sell to Specific Needs

In order to make presentations interesting, points of discussion need to relate to the needs, curiosities, and interests of the audience. Instead of delivering a canned presentation, presenters should base their agenda on the needs and problems identified in pre-presentation conversations, site visits, and questionnaires. Presentation content should match specific buyer needs, pains, and problems to proposed product or service solutions.

When presenters deliver need-based presentations, rather than generic presentations, buyers associate value with the proposed product or service. When sellers cater presentations to the specific needs and interests of buyers, solutions not only become more obvious, they become more appealing.

This is why pre-presentation site visits, questionnaires, and needs-analysis discussions are so important. They equip presenters with account specific information that can be used to create presentation content and to deliver needs-based solutions. By uncovering critical needs and problems to solve, presenters create consultative relationships with buyers and increase the likelihood of making a successful presentation.

Commandment 5: Make Memorable Introductions and Conclusions

The saying, "first impressions are lasting impressions" is true. In the first moments of a presentation, participants are alert, attentive, and focused on the presenter. The introduction is one of the few portions of the presentation in which presenters have the undivided attention of audience participants. It is the perfect opportunity for presenters to start off with a bang.

Because the first few minutes of a presentation burn a lasting impression on the minds of participants, and because the beginning of a presentation sets the tone for the remainder of the presentation, getting off on the right foot is important to delivering a successful presentation.

Winning presenters create winning introductions. They answer fundamental questions that buyers ask in the first few minutes of a presentation. Using a simple five-step process, winning presenters introduce themselves, refer to a timeframe, set an agenda, provide a corporate capabilities statement, and quickly review client needs (see Chapter 8). By implementing these five steps, presenters cover all the bases of an effective introduction.

Effective conclusions are equally important. Because the conclusion is what participants hear last, it is important to close the presentation with a powerful and memorable message.

Research confirms that audience participants remember the beginning and the end of a presentation more than the middle. They also remember the end of a presentation more than the beginning. That means that regardless of how effective a presenter is in the introduction and body of a presentation, if the close is weak, that's what the audience will remember. It is critical, therefore, to end a presentation with a powerful conclusion.

The four steps to a powerful conclusion are ending on time, summarizing hot points and competitive differential advantages, concluding with a compelling closing sentence, and transitioning buyers to the closing stage of the sales cycle (see Chapter 10).

The Point? Effective introductions and conclusions make lasting impressions on buyers. They are the most memorable part of a presentation and need to be well planned and well delivered.

Commandment 6: Present with Passion

Remember Patrick Henry's "Liberty or Death" speech? What made it so memorable? What made it so effective? One word: Passion.

There are many attributes that successful presenters have in common. Passion is one of them. Passion creates a sense of believability in the presenter and the presented product. When a presenter delivers a message with passion, buyers feel that the presenter truly believes in the product or service being offered.

Like Patrick Henry's speech, passionate presenters create energy, stimulate the thoughts and emotions of buyers, and fully engage participants. They create a sense of excitement and urgency associated with their product or service. Non-passionate presenters are boring, indifferent, and do not project confidence in their product or service.

It is difficult to exaggerate the importance of showing passion in a sales presentation. The primary reason is that passion sells. It creates a sense of believability. Passionate presenters radiate genuine belief in the value of the products or services being presented. They communicate confidence in their proposed solutions. When presenters show genuine enthusiasm for their product or service, buyers add significance to the proposed goods and services. The bottom line is, presenters who show passion are more believable and, therefore, more successful.

Commandment 7: Focus on Benefits

I reviewed a full-page advertisement in *USA Today*. In big, bold lettering the ad said, "Whiter teeth. Healthier gums." That was it. At the bottom of the ad was a small picture of a Phillips Sonicare toothbrush. The caption below the picture read, "The sonic toothbrush." Phillips wasn't selling a toothbrush. It was selling the benefits of using the toothbrush.

Focusing on product or service benefits and not features is a universally accepted presentation principle. Unfortunately, it is also a universally ignored principle. It is too often ignored, not because presenters disagree with the advice, but because many presenters do not know *how* to implement the advice.

The first step to focusing on benefits and not features is identifying the needs, pains, and problems of potential buyers. Conducting a thorough client needs-analysis prior to the presentation is critical. Once a presenter has identified client needs and problems, he or she can match specific product or service capabilities to the identified needs and problems. A simple and effective way to do this is with *The Needs-Resolution Matrix* (see Chapter 12). *The Needs-Resolution Matrix* helps presenters to apply specific product capabilities to exact buyer problems. Using *The Needs-Resolution Matrix*, salespeople present products and services in a way that clearly demonstrates the benefits of applying the proposed product or service. It also prevents presenters from engaging in low level "feature wars" that distract buyers from focusing on the benefits of implementing the proposed product or service.

The second way to focus on benefits instead of features is to use scenarios that buyers can relate to. By using realistic scenarios and graphic illustrations of participants (or existing clients) using the product or service, presenters drive home the benefits of implementing the solution. Keep in mind that graphs, charts, and statistics do not move people. Scenarios, stories, and examples do. Dramatize benefits with stories and scenarios.

> **Note:** People don't buy features. They buy benefits. Product features are meaningless unless they help buyers fill needs or eliminate pain. Focus on the benefits of products and services, not features.

Asking effective solution-benefit questions is also a way to emphasize benefits and not features. Solution-benefit questions help buyers focus on the value of solving problems and resolving pains. They center on the benefits of the presented solution and move prospects from recognizing the implications of the current problems to focusing on the benefits of the proposed solution. Solution-benefit questions emphasize the positive benefits of solving identified problems with questions such as, "What benefits do you see from implementing X capability?" "What benefits do you see from resolving Y issue?" Or, "How valuable would it be for you to be able to eliminate ABC problem?" All of these questions focus buyers on the benefits associated with product or service implementation instead of product or service features.

For ultimate impact, presentation messages should focus on the benefits buyers will experience from implementing presented products or services. By doing so, presenters demonstrate to buyers the benefits associated with product implementation and the value of the proposed purchase.

Commandment 8: Get Serious about Using Humor

There is nothing worse than sitting through a presentation that is dry, solemn, or "as serious as a heart attack." Presenters who fail to weave a few funny one liners or humorous stories into their presentation not only bypass one of the most effective communication tools known to man, they also deliver less effective presentations.

The primary benefit of using humor is likeability. Audiences tend to like presenters who use humor. Presenters who inject funny one-liners, self-effacing humor, or amusing stories are not only more entertaining, they are also more engaging. Their friendliness, charm, or wit make them more likeable and, therefore, more believable. People are far more favorably disposed toward presenters who have a sense of humor than toward presenters who are somber and humorless.

Anyone can learn to use humor effectively. You don't have to be a comedian or be "naturally" funny to inject humor into a presentation. Some of the funniest one-liners in Hollywood come from one of the most serious faces in the movie industry—Arnold Schwarzenegger. Who can forget, "Hasta la vista, baby!"? To use humor effectively, you simply have to have a *sense* of humor. You have to be able to recognize good humor and use it.

Some of the easiest forms of humor to use in a presentation include:

Humorous Stories and Funny Quotes—Humorous stories can be found in magazines such as *Readers Digest* or on the Internet. Simply type in "humorous stories" or "clean jokes" in any major search engine, and you will find hundreds of websites that offer thousands of jokes, stories, quotes, definitions, and other humorous material that can be used in a presentation.

Cartoons—Cartoons are great sources of humor. The funny pages of any major newspaper offer cartoons that can relate to most presentation topics. The Internet also provides Web sites that offer humorous cartoons. Most cartoons can be downloaded (at a cost) or "copied and pasted" into PowerPoint slide presentations.

Self-effacing Humor—There is a saying that, "You can build yourself up by putting yourself down." Most highly skilled presenters share a common trait—a good sense of humor and the ability to direct it at themselves. Poking a little fun at yourself reflects confidence and is one of the safest forms of presentation humor.

Magic Tricks—Magic tricks are fantastic tools for entertaining an audience, getting people to smile, and even making a serious point. You don't have to be a professional magician to use magic tricks. The key is finding a magic trick that is easy to demonstrate. Go to your local hobby store or magic shop, tell them what you are attempting to accomplish, and get their advice. They will have recommendations for magic tricks that you can use in a presentation environment.

> **The Point?** Use humor to build likeability, engage audiences, reduce tension, and enhance the presentation experience.

Commandment 9: Utilize Presentation Assistants

When Julius Caesar invaded Britain in 55 B.C., his Roman soldiers encountered Celtic warriors skilled in chariot warfare. The Celtic warriors would attack their opponents by maneuvering their chariots close enough to their enemies to hurl javelins and shoot arrows. They would then leap from their chariots to fight hand to hand with broadsword, axe, and shield. When wearied from battle, the Celtic warrior would whistle to his servant (called a charioteer) who would then swing the chariot in and pick him up. The speed and skill of the warrior's charioteer in maneuvering the chariot was often the difference between life and death.

When possible, presenters should use assistants to help with the duties of conducting a successful presentation. Presentation assistants can take care of logistical matters so that presenters can focus exclusively on presentation content and delivery.

In committee-based presentations that involve multiple buyers and complex technology, technical assistants and sales engineers are often necessary for set-up, demonstrations, and answering complicated technical questions.

The presentation assistant's duties might include:

- Setting up and testing technical equipment
- Testing audio-visual equipment
- Setting up seating arrangements
- Greeting and seating participants
- Distributing handouts and presentation literature
- Introducing the presenter
- Adjusting lighting and acoustics
- Controlling the room temperature
- Timing the presentation
- Providing feedback on delivery, content, and visuals aids
- Assisting with visuals during the presentation
- Addressing questions after the presentation

Presentation assistants offer an added benefit: they help build and maintain the confidence of the presenter. Having a competent presentation assistant boosts the comfort and confidence of a presenter and helps prevent him or her from feeling isolated and alone.

Commandment 10: Have High expectations

Whether you think you can or you think you can't, you're probably right.

—Henry Ford

Studies indicate that a presenter's expectations and attitude prior to presenting are accurate predictors of the outcome of the presentation. Research has shown that presenters with high expectations are more successful than those with lower expectations. They typically get what they expect. Presenters who predict being successful usually are.

The essence of this phenomenon is captured in the saying, "Success breeds success." People tend to expect what they experience. People who are highly successful expect to be successful. People who are moderately successful expect to be moderately successful. People who are failures more often than not expect to fail. The key to achieving success is building success one step at a time. The more success a person experiences, the more success a person expects. Presenters with high ambitions typically get what they set out to achieve.[1]

In Summary

The Ten Commandments of Presenting are:

1. Be Prepared
2. Rehearse, Rehearse, Rehearse
3. Create a Presentation Outline
4. Avoid Generic Presentations—Sell To Specific Needs
5. Make Memorable Introduction and Conclusions
6. Present With Passion
7. Focus on Benefits
8. Get Serious About Using Humor
9. Utilize Presentation Assistants
10. Have High Expectations

---

1. For an excellent analysis on success, see *Success Is A Choice*, by Rick Pitino, Broadway Books, 1997.

Chapter 18

Implementing Winning Sales Presentation Skills

Far better it is to dare mighty things, to win glorious triumphs, even though checkered by failure, than to take rank with those poor spirits who neither enjoy much nor suffer much, because they live in the grey twilight that knows not victory nor defeat.

—Teddy Roosevelt

On June 24, 1314, King Edward II of England led a vast army to the banks of a small stream in Scotland called the Bannockburn to crush the Scottish fight for independence. Standing in his way was the newly appointed King of Scotland, Robert Bruce. Fearing the growing numbers of Scottish highlanders joining Bruce's ranks, and knowing of their tenacity in battle, Edward II summoned a massive group of mercenaries and English troops to defeat the defiant Scots. He hired knights from France and Germany, infantry from Ireland, famed archers from Wales, and was able to bribe and lure thousands of Scotsmen who opposed Bruce into his army. It was the largest army ever assembled by a king of England and consisted of close to 25,000 men.

Bruce's army numbered between 5,000 and 6,000 troops, the majority of whom were Highlanders accustomed to mountain fighting, and no cavalry to speak of. They were, however, armed with something much more powerful than horses or guns. They were armed with a determination fed by an angered populace aroused by English cruelty.

In an attempt to bolster the spirit of his men, Bruce summoned his officers and gave them their order of battle.

> We have every reason to be confident of our success for we have right on our side. Our enemies are moved only by desire for dominion but we are fighting for our lives, our children, our wives, and the free-

> dom of our country. And so I ask and pray that with all your strength, without cowardice or alarm, you meet the foes whom you will first encounter so boldly that those behind them will tremble. See that your ranks are not broken so that, when the enemy come charging on horseback, you meet them steadfastly with your spears... Think on your manhood and your deeds of valor and the joy that awaits you if you are victorious. In your hands you carry honor, praise, riches, freedom and felicity if you bear yourselves bravely, but altogether to the contrary if your hearts fail you. You could have lived quietly as slaves, but because you longed to be free you are with me here, and to gain that end you must be valiant, strong, and undismayed.

The officers then returned to their men to tell them what the King had said and prepared them for the morrow.

Early the next morning, the English army began parading toward the Scots. As they approached, Scottish soldiers watched in amazement. They had never seen such a multitude of military splendor and might. In an act of desperate piety, the Scottish soldiers knelt in unison and made a short prayer to God to help them in the fight. Seeing the Scottish soldiers kneel, Edward II exclaimed triumphantly, "They kneel for mercy!" To which his aide de camp replied, "For mercy yes, but not from you—from God for their sins. These men will win all or die."

As the English vanguard began positioning its attack, one of its knights, Sir Henry de Bohun, rode boastfully on a powerful horse and carrying a large lance in his hand in front of the army clad in full armor. As he entered the open field on the north bank of the Bannockburn, he recognized the King of the Scots and with lightning speed, turned his horse and spurred toward him. Bruce, seeing Bohun charging toward him, wheeled his horse around and charged back. The two knights rushed toward each other in open battle in front of thousands of onlooking troops. As the horses thundered toward each other, Bohun lifted his joust, Bruce his battle-axe. As they drew near, Bruce suddenly swerved to one side and, rising in his stirrups, brought his axe down with such force that it cut through Bohun's armor and killed him.

Stunned silence momentarily ensued. Then, suddenly, a wild scream filled the air as the Highlander foot soldiers attacked the English cavalry. Inspired by the boldness of their leader, and following his example, the Highlanders took the offensive. They attacked with such speed and ferocity that many of the English knights fled. Shocked at the sight of an oncoming attack, the entire English vanguard was put to flight.

Outnumbered, starved, and poorly equipped, Robert Bruce led his beloved Scots to victory. His physical courage, strength in adversity, resourcefulness in danger, brilliance in tactic, and unmatched perseverance won, not only the battle of Bannockburn, but also the freedom of his people.

The historic lesson contained in this experience is this: Those who wait tend to relax and become careless. Those who act, and work hard to improve their situation, become more skilled, and more successful.

From Theory to Application

At the conclusion of our presentation trainings, I am consistently asked, "How do we implement your training? How do we convert theory into practice? Is there a way for us to turn board room trainings into practical application?"

There is, of course, no easy answer to these questions. Understanding does not necessarily translate into *doing*. However, there are some fundamental guidelines that will speed up the implementation of winning presentation principles.

Once individuals have mastered the ideas and concepts in *Winning Sales Presentations,* it is critical to channel the newly acquired information into habits.[1] I have identified five implementation rules that follow skill-learning principles:

- Focus on one skill at a time
- Focus on quantity, not quality
- Set goals and standards
- Plan
- Don't become discouraged

Focus on One Skill at a Time

In 890, Alfred the Great identified seven maxims that he strove to follow. He then worked on each behavior individually. Benjamin Franklin did much the same in 1771. He outlined thirteen virtues that "occurred to me as necessary or desirable." Franklin then set aside time to focus on each virtue separately. "I determined to give a week's strict attention to each of the virtues successively. Thus, in the first week, my great guard was to avoid every day the least offense against temperance [his first virtue]... Proceeding thus to the last, I could get through a course complete in thirteen weeks and four courses a year. And like him who, having a garden to weed, does not attempt to eradicate all the bad herbs at once... but works on one of the beds at a time, and having accomplished the first, proceeds to the second."[2]

1. *Patrick Henry & Associates,* has systematized an implementation program that can be customized to the needs of individuals and organizations. To learn how to best implement winning presentation skills and strategies for your business or situation, contact *Patrick Henry & Associates,* toll-free (877) 204-4341.

2. *The Autobiography of Benjamin Franklin* (New York: Barnes and Noble Books, 1994) 106-108.

Basketball coach Pat Riley outlined in his book, *The Winner Within*, a program that he used with the Los Angeles Lakers to break down complex skills into component behaviors. "From a list of fifteen possible measures, we selected five that had really cost us the last championship. These defined five 'trigger points,' five areas which comprised the basis of basketball performance for each role and position. We challenged each player to put forth enough effort to gain just one percentage point in each of those five areas."[3] He then focused on each skill, one at a time, with each player. The result? The next year, the Lakers won the NBA championship.

When softball players work on hitting, they don't attempt to work on their throwing skills at the same time. They focus on one skill at a time. Like successful athletes, successful presenters do not work on multiple skills simultaneously. They isolate a particular skill and work on it. After mastering the targeted skill, they move on to the next skill.

The Point? Center on one skill at a time and hammer it. Work on it. Think about it. Write it down. Practice it. Concentrate your efforts on developing one skill at a time.

Focus on Quantity, Not Quality

As a young man, I had a basketball coach teach me how to shoot free throws. He showed me the correct mechanics of shooting—bringing my elbow up to a square position, bending my shooting wrist back, following through, etc. After teaching me the correct way to shoot, he then said, "Now go shoot 100 free throws and come back and talk to me again." He understood quantity would lead to quality.

Patrick Henry & Associates, refers to this skill learning concept as *The Quantity Principle. The Quantity Principle* instructs students to focus on the quantity of the skill versus the quality of the skill. New

3. Pat Riley, *The Winner Within* (New York: Berkley Books, 1993) 163.

behaviors are learned through a *quantity* of repetition and practice. Quality comes with time. As new behaviors are learned, adjustments will be made, and skills will be refined. The important part of skill learning is doing, practicing, engaging.

> **Caution!** In the initial stages of skill learning, don't worry about perfection. Don't worry about making mistakes. Don't worry about quality. Focus on *quantity* and quality will follow.

Set Goals and Standards

A goal is a desired objective used to motivate and enhance a person's ability to succeed. Goals give people direction and focus and are essential to improving performance.

Setting and achieving goals is not a trivial process. It takes good data, good thinking, and good instincts to set good goals. Inappropriate goals can actually have an adverse effect on a person's performance. Unrealistically high goals that are not achievable not only fail to motivate, they actually de-motivate people by making them feel unsuccessful. Goals that are too easy to achieve, on the other hand, do not inspire people to stretch and grow.

A seller who wants to improve his or her selling skills can set a goal to memorize two questions from each category of *The DNASelling Method*, or he or she can create a corporate capabilities statement. By setting goals, sellers motivate themselves to improve their presentation skills.

The most important aspect of a goal is its means of fulfillment. After establishing a goal, it is necessary that a process of accomplishment be set up to implement it. Why? Because without clearly identifying steps of achievement, people don't have goals—they have hopes.

A *goal* is an objective. A *standard* is a means of achieving the objective. Goals without standards are like weight loss programs without exercise. An example of a *goal* is to try to lose twenty pounds. An example of a *standard* is to work out every morning from 6:30 to

7:00. Standards are like "mini goals" that are fulfilled on a daily or weekly basis that map a clear path to goal achievement.

When setting goals, set personal standards to achieve the goals.

> **The Point?** Develop goals and standards that are challenging, motivating, and achievable.

Plan

You've undoubtedly heard Benjamin Franklin's oft-repeated maxim, "By failing to prepare, you are preparing to fail." This dictum is scripture in the business world. Plan ahead. Schedule specific dates, times, and accounts to implement your new skills.

In order to present well, you must first plan well. Strategic planning is the cornerstone of successful presentations. If you don't have an effective plan for presenting, any success you experience is purely accidental. Use the tools provided in this book to plan your presentations in advance. Anticipate possible problems or potential resistance. Create an outline. Develop rich content. Plan and analyze the implementation of your newly acquired skills and knowledge. Analyze your presentations.

What went well?

What could I have done differently?

Did I address the needs of the presentation participants?

What benefits had the greatest influence?

What skills could I have implemented?

The key to implementation is to plan and schedule. Map out where work is needed. Week one: Identifying buyer needs. Week two: Creating better conclusions, etc.

Don't Become Discouraged

A smooth sea never made a skilled mariner.
—English Proverb

In 1832, Abraham Lincoln lost his job in a failing business partnership. Also in 1832, he was defeated for the state legislature. In 1833, his private business failed. Although elected to the state legislature in 1834, he implemented an internal improvement project that nearly bankrupted the State of Illinois. He was defeated twice for the house speaker position in 1836 and 1838. In 1843, Lincoln was defeated for the nomination to the U.S. Congress. Although elected to congress in 1846, he lost the renomination in 1848. The year 1849 saw Lincoln run for a land-office position and lose. In 1854, he was defeated for the U.S. Senate. In 1856, Lincoln was defeated for the nomination for Vice-President, and, in 1858, repeated his losing bid for the U.S. Senate. In 1860, he was elected President of The United States of America.

Achieving excellence is a journey, not a destination. It's a voyage wrought with bumps and bruises. As Abraham Lincoln's experience illustrates, bouts of failure are part of the path of success. Setbacks and mistakes come with the territory. It's part of the process. The key is to learn from mistakes and failures and take the lessons to heart.

Many professionals learn new and better ways of presenting but don't convert the newly acquired knowledge into habits because they become discouraged. Give new skills a chance. No new skill feels natural the first time you use it. It may initially feel a bit awkward and artificial. That's perfectly normal, so don't quit after only a few attempts. Keep working on it. Role-play it, think about it, practice it. Don't become discouraged.

Presentation Success—Deserve It.

There never has been devised, and there never will be devised, any law which will enable a man to succeed save by the exercise of those qualities which have always been the prerequisites of success—the qualities of hard work, of keen intelligence, of unflinching will.

—Teddy Roosevelt

Success in any endeavor must be earned. There is no magic potion. In order to be successful, sellers must pay the price. They must sow before they reap. They must deserve success.

Winning presenters follow a simple success equation:

Winning Presentation Skills x Work = Success

Goals cannot be wish lists. They have to be work lists. Thinking about your dreams is rarely enough to create the habits to fulfill them. While it is good to start with dreams and goals, before any of your dreams and goals can be realized, you must first deserve your success by acquiring selling skills and working hard. By combining old-fashioned work habits with winning presentation skills, you will be equipped with the tools to consistently win.

If you want to succeed—deserve success.

No one can guarantee success in war—one can only deserve it.

—Winston Churchill

The Point? You can do it. Be *patiently persistent* and your skills will improve. Persevere and your selling success will increase. Follow *Winning Presentation* principles, work hard and you will be successful. You will have earned it.

The SONAR Selling System

The SONAR Selling System is a comprehensive selling process and development curriculum that implements contemporary prospecting, selling, presenting, and negotiating skills. Coupled with good Lead Generation and CRM technology, *The SONAR Selling System* equips individuals and organizations with the skills, strategies, and technology to fill pipelines with qualified leads and win more sales.

The SONAR Selling System is a holistic sales and marketing approach validated for helping sales professionals and organizations achieve optimum performance. Based on the philosophy that selling is a science, an observable, verifiable, and measurable process, *The SONAR Selling System* equips clients with the skills, strategies, and technology to increase sales, measure results, and accurately forecast revenue projections.

The SONAR Selling System is the only comprehensive and fully integrated sales performance development model available. Each skill process works seamlessly with others through shared approaches, language, and technology. Sales professionals and organizations trained in *The SONAR Selling System* improve performance, outperform competitors, and increase bottom-line profitability.

Patrick Henry & Associates

Patrick Henry & Associates is a performance development company that coaches individuals and companies to dramatically increase sales revenue.

Each skill related component of *The SONAR Selling System* has an associated book and integrated performance-based curriculum designed for personal, corporate, and executive trainings.

Corporate Training

Patrick Henry & Associates offers the following training programs:

Power Prospecting teaches a structured process for script development, pipeline management, and telephone interaction to generate new leads, set appointments, and fill pipelines with qualified opportunities.

The DNASelling Method provides a systematic approach to selling that improves questioning skills, differentiates presented solutions from competing products, and gains commitment with effective closing strategies.

Winning Sales Presentations instructs business leaders and salespeople in a five-step process *(The Presentation Pedigree)* to prepare strategic content, master effective communication skills, and deliver exceptional presentations.

Sales-Side Negotiation trains business executives and sales professionals to build, balance, and maintain power, recognize and overcome negotiation tactics, minimize discounts, negotiate favorable agreements, and develop mutually beneficial relationships.

Each module of *The SONAR Selling System* has a corporate training program with a one to two day initial training, followed by a structured field application process. An optional one-day mastery workshop is conducted after field application for follow up, skill reinforcement, and permanent change.

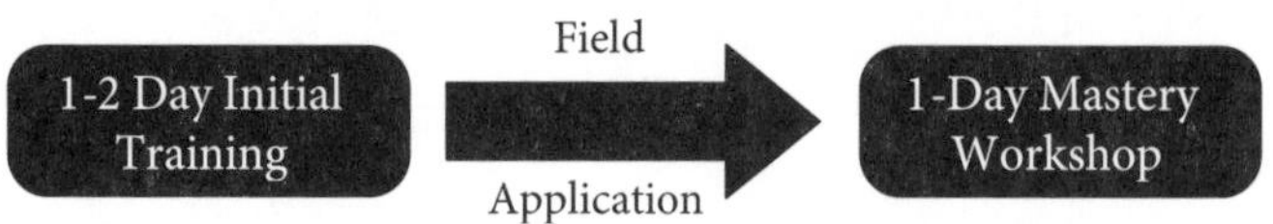

Executive Retreats

For account executives, managers, directors, vice presidents, presidents, CEO's, and other business leaders, *Patrick Henry & Associates* offers executive retreats. Using "train the trainer" methods, *Patrick Henry & Associates* instructs business leaders in *The SONAR Selling System* and equips them with the skills and strategies to incorporate *The Selling System* in their own business or sales organization.

Executive retreats are conducted at prestigious locations around the world and include afternoon and weekend options of fly-fishing, golfing, skiing, hiking, biking, sightseeing, and other recreational activities.

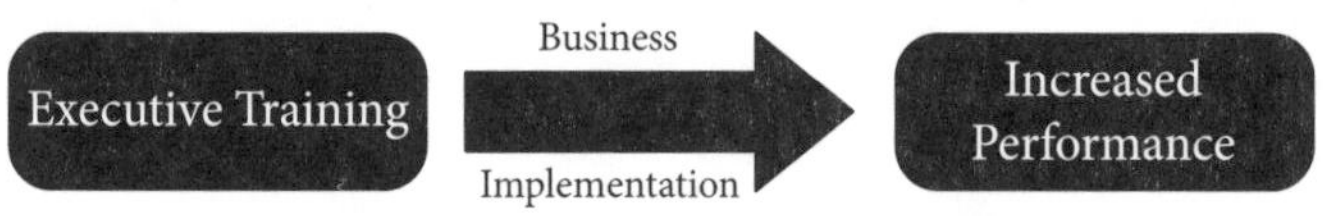

Speeches and Seminars

Patrick Henry & Associates provides speeches and seminars that can be customized to specific audiences, companies, or industries. For more details concerning public seminars, key note speeches, corporate trainings, and executive retreats that teach, train, and certify sales professionals, managers, and executives in *The SONAR Selling System*, contact:

Patrick Henry & Associates, Inc.
1831 Fort Union Blvd. Suite 210
Salt Lake City, Utah 84121
www.PatrickHenryInc.com
1 (877) 204-4341

Selected Bibliography

Adams, Jeremy, Wick Allison, and Gavin Hambly. *Condemned to Repeat It*. New York: Penguin Books, 1998.

Ambrose, Stephen E., *Undaunted Courage*. New York: Simon & Schuster, 1996.

Axelrod, Alan. *Elizabeth I, CEO*. New York: Prentice Hall Press, 2000.

—. *Profiles in Leadership*. New York: Prentice Hall Press, 2003.

Banfield, Susan. *Joan of Arc*. New York: Burke Publishing Company, 1988.

Bailey, Thomas, and David Kennedy. *The American Pageant*. Lexington: Heath and Company, 1991.

Beyer, Rick. *The Greatest Stories Never Told*. New York: Harper Collins, 2003.

Boritt, Gabor. *Why The Confederacy Lost*. New York: Oxford University Press, 1992.

Boyd, Katherine, and Bruce Lenman. *Larouse Dictionary of World History*. New York: Chambers Harrap Publishers, 1993.

Caesar, Gaius Julius. *The Conquest of Gaul*. Translated by S.A. Hanford. New York: Penguin Books, 1982.

Campbell, Dickson Norine. *Patrick Henry: Patriot And Statesman*. Old Greenwhich: The Devin-Adair Company, 1969.

Churchill, Winston S. *History Of The English-Speaking Peoples*. New York: Wings Books, 1994.

Corvisier, Andre. *A Dictionary of Military History*. Translated by Chris Turner. Cambridge: Blackwell Publishers, 1994.

Franklin, Benjamin. *The Autobiography of Benjamin Franklin*. New York: Barnes & Noble Books, 1994.

Grafton, Johne. *Abraham Lincoln: Great Speeches*. New York: Dover Publications, 1991.

Greene, Robert, and Joost Elffers. *The 48 Laws Of Power*. New York: Penguin Books, 2000.

Helm, P. H. *Alfred The Great*. New York: Barnes & Noble Books, 1995.

Jacobson, Julius H., *The Classical Music Experience.* New York: Sourcebooks, 2002.

Jimenez, Ramon. *Caesar Against The Celts.* New York: Sarpedon, 1996.

MacArthur, Brian. *The Penguin Book Of Historic Speeches.* New York: Penguin Books, 1996.

Rand, Clayton. *Sons Of The South.* New York: Holt, Rinehart and Winston, 1961.

Ritchie, W.F. *Celtic Warriors.* Buckinghamshire: Shire Publications, 1997.

Roosevelt, Theodore. *The Strenuous Life.* Bedford: Applewood Books, 1991.

Scott, Ronald McNair. *Robert The Bruce.* New York: Peter Bedrick Books, 1989.

Shirer, William. *The Rise And Fall Of The Third Reich.* New York: Simon Schuster, 1960.

Snyder, Louis. *Great Turning Points In History.* New York: Barnes & Noble Books, 1996.

Sun Tzu. *The Art of War.* Translated by Ralph D. Sawyer. New York: Barnes & Noble Books, 1994.

Index

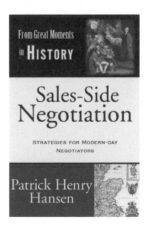

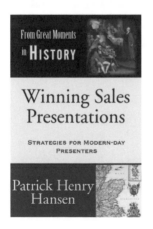

About The Author

Patrick Henry Hansen is the founder of *Patrick Henry & Associates* and is the creator of *The SONAR Selling System, The DNASelling Method,* and *SONAR* technology. His organization provides sales process optimization, corporate trainings, and executive retreats for sales managers, coaches, and leaders. Mr. Hansen is the author of numerous books and is considered one of the foremost authorities on sales methodology, sales-side negotiation, and business strategy. Mr. Hansen is a popular speaker, consultant, and educator, and has trained, coached, and influenced thousands of professionals in winning presentation principles.

Prior to starting *Patrick Henry & Associates,* Mr. Hansen was a sales representative, manager, and executive. As an executive for multiple technology companies, he introduced advanced selling systems that increased sales more than 100% in each company.

Mr. Hansen founded *The Business America Radio Show,* received his BA from Brigham Young University and currently resides in Salt Lake City, Utah with his wife Laura and their five children.

Refer questions to:

Patrick Henry & Associates, Inc.
1831 Fort Union Blvd., Suite 210
Salt Lake City, Utah 84121
Phone: 1 (877) 204-4341
Fax: 1 (877) 204-4341
www.PatrickHenryInc.com

From Great Moments in History **Book Series ($14.95 each)**

# of copies

_____ *Power Prospecting*: Cold Calling Strategies for Modern-day Sales People

_____ *The DNASelling Method*: Strategies for Modern-day Sales People

_____ *Winning Sales Presentations*: Strategies for Modern-day Presenters

_____ *Sales-Side Negotiation*: Strategies for Modern-day Negotiators

_____ S/H Add $4.00 for shipping & handling (up to 4 books)

_____ Tax Sales Tax (Utah Residents 6.25%)

_____ Total

Name: ____________________

Company: ____________________

Business Address: ____________________

City, State, Zip: ____________________

Phone: ____________________

email: ____________________

Payment: Cash ____ Check ____ Charge ____ (MasterCard, Visa or American Express)

Acct. # ____________________

Expiration Date: __________

Signature ____________________

Please make your check payable & return to:

Patrick Henry & Associates
1831 Fort Union Blvd. STE 210
Salt Lake City, Utah 84121

Call your credit card order to: 877-204-4341 or order online at: www.patrickhenryinc.com